Creating the Ultimate Workplace Performance Management System

Why Traditional Performance Appraisals Don't Work

by

Matthew Savino
B.A., L.L.B. C.H.R.E.

Introduction

Creating the Ultimate Workplace Performance Management System
Why Traditional Performance Appraisals Don't Work
By Matthew Savino, B.A., LL.B., C.H.R.E
Sentinel Management Publishing, Copyright 2019, 2015.
All Rights Reserved

Creating the Ultimate Workplace Performance Management System
is based on Matthew's personally developed training program, which
he has implemented in numerous workplaces over the course of a 20-
year career as a Vice President of Human Resources and Management
Consultant. As the Principal and Founder of *SHRP Limited,* and co-
Founder of the software-as-a-service company *HRLive,* Matthew
has successfully implemented this program with clients in both
public and private sectors, and is now making it available to any
business or organizational leader who would like to develop and
optimize their own in-house performance management system.

Comments from clients who have worked with Matthew:

*"The great thing about Matthew's program is that it can be adapted to
companies and organizations of any size. The principles of goal setting,
employee engagement, and how to retain your top performers are as relevant
to a business with 10 employees as they are to a multi-national organization
of thousands."*

Michael J. Lord, President & CEO
Gilead Power Corporation

"As Managers we all feel that we know how to deliver constructive feedback and how to lead an effective performance discussion, but Matthew has some really useful tips to help structure these type of interactions in a positive way. We all need a reminder from time to time that it's not about what you say, but how you say it!"

Ron Greer, CEO
Ryder Material Handling

"Matthew's program is adaptable to almost any business or organization, regardless of the number of employees. We appreciated his common-sense approach to the employee issues that managers and business owners face every day. His program will continue to guide our performance management practices as we grow."

John Desbiens, President & CEO
Cambium Inc.

Contents

PART I

Performance Management, A Step-By-Step Guide

Chapter 1:

Setting Yourself Up for Success

*"The type of person you are is
usually reflected in your business.
To improve your business, first
improve yourself."* Idowu Koyenikan,
Wealth for All: Living a Life of
Success at the Edge of Your Ability

As a leader within your organization, you have a vested interest in achieving goals and aiming for success. Your bottom line depends on it. Don't assume, however, that every person you hire will share your passion for achievement. An employee's day-to-day activities are not always automatically linked to organizational goals and values. While some employees will have an innate desire to make the most of each work day, others will need additional motivational cues to reach the optimal performance levels that you would like to see them achieve. You need to establish a system to ensure your team understands what is important to you, and to your organization. Don't assume your employees know what you are thinking!

While more money and extra vacation days are appreciated universally, they are not necessarily the core solution for creating a high-performance team. What motivates a person can be a complicated matter, and a question to which there cannot be one definitive answer. Determining which motivators will keep your staff engaged and enthusiastic about their work is an ongoing process, based on a constructive dialogue that should occur on a continuous basis.

This is why having a structured Performance Management System in place is so critical to your organization's success. A business is only as strong as its least engaged team member: the people you are working with are absolutely instrumental to the sustainability of your enterprise, and all it takes are a few weak links to undermine an otherwise solid foundation. Every member of your team must work together cohesively towards a common goal – but are you sure they know what that goal is?

It is not enough to give your staff a list of objectives or targets that they are expected to achieve. In the long term no one responds well to "Do This" commands, even if there is a financial reward at the end. They must be a part of the goal-setting process. They must truly *want* to do a good job. You cannot instantly queue intrinsic motivation in your employees, but you can create the conditions in your workplace that will foster an environment to inspire that unique and absolutely essential type of engagement.

The Canadian Federation of Independent Business (often referred to as the "voice for small business" in Canada), published a survey in which two thirds of their members identified employees as the most important element in their success – more important, even, than the product or service they sell. That is a remarkable observation.

Regrettably, two thirds of respondents also indicated they are experiencing difficulties recruiting and engaging qualified staff for their businesses. This shortage is continuing to grow. Interestingly, a lack of experience didn't concern these employers – in fact, small employers spend billions on training to address experience and skill gaps. Their larger concern was a lack of enthusiasm and engagement amongst candidates and employees. That represents a significant problem for small and medium-sized organizations. While this survey canvassed small businesses only, I expect these concerns relate to larger employers as well.

The employee engagement gap is a much more complex issue to address than a skills or experience gap, and the investment of financial resources alone cannot resolve this issue. As many as 60 per cent of Canada's jobs are in small or medium-sized enterprises, so these observations have substantial implications for the national workforce and economy.

The program outlined in this book will help you to use communication, goal setting, development strategies and constructive feedback to optimize the performance of your staff, and to create a team environment where everyone understands how important their performance is to their co-workers, to management, and to the success of your enterprise as a whole. Employee engagement has never been more important, or more under threat, than it is now in our modern workplace.

The main purpose of performance management, as we will establish it, is to achieve results for your organization by:

- ❖ understanding and leveraging motivation

- ❖ setting goals and expectations

- ❖ monitoring progress and providing feedback

- ❖ cultivating skills and aptitude

- ❖ assessing performance

- ❖ improving performance, and

- ❖ recognizing and rewarding accomplishments.

The History of Performance Systems

Performance evaluations and performance management systems have been around a long time and find their earliest origins in third century China, though the concept of conducting performance evaluations was not popularized until the Industrial Revolution. By the 1950's, Peter Drucker (the Austrian-born management consultant, professor, and author) established a "management by objectives" approach which still forms the centerpiece of many organizations' performance systems. While Drucker's core value of respecting the worker spoke to many, his "management by objectives" concept has been widely criticized as overemphasizing control, as opposed to fostering creativity among workers. With top-down assessments, rating scales and one-way feedback, it is understandable that traditional performance management systems have developed a bad rap over the years.

Stanford University Professor Bob Sutton[1] has said that doing performance evaluations is like *"blood-letting – it is a bad practice that does more harm than good in all or nearly all cases"* – leaving many to conclude that the negative feedback associated with evaluations leads to a self-fulfilling prophecy: the employee who receives a poor evaluation does even worse in the subsequent rating period.

A group of HR Executives in the US gave their own performance review systems a lacklustre "C" grading and a study of some 600 feedback systems found that two thirds of them had a "zero" or worse still, a negative impact on employee performance[2]. Half of the respondents to a Mercer report, *Global Performance Management Survey[3]*, indicated their system needed an overhaul and only three percent indicated their system delivered "exceptional value". Three percent is not exactly a convincing victory.

Performance Management Defined

Before we go further we should define the term "Performance Management". Performance Management as we will define it includes a series of techniques and interventions that are aimed at improving, developing and sustaining performance. There are two complementary, but quite distinctive streams of activity within this definition of a performance management system.

"Performance Development" is, as the name suggests, squarely aimed at growth and employee improvement. Many organizations have performance evaluation or appraisal systems which they believe develop performance. In fact, these systems typically deliver constructive feedback and other corrective actions that target an improvement in performance or behavior. Performance development is (or should be) purely aimed at growing and enhancing the capabilities of your employees. While there is a time and place for critical feedback, the development discussion is not it. Regrettably, many annual performance appraisals become encumbered with the stigma of one-way feedback that eliminates the opportunity to inspire the employee. This is why so many employees await the annual review process with anxiety, and managers alike share the reticence of having to deliver the bad news along with the good.

Performance correction is a necessary tool in a complete system of performance management. However, corrective measures used to address gaps in performance should be contemporaneously applied at the time when the gap or conduct issue is observed. *Do not employ corrective action in conjunction with a development discussion.* Performance development is a distinct and potentially powerful opportunity to foster growth and to instill a profound level of engagement. However, if you simultaneously pursue performance correction activities, you will undermine the impact and potency of any development opportunity.

Effective performance management demands the active pursuit of both of the intervention streams noted above. However, though they may be complementary and essential to a comprehensive performance management system, they are not the same – nor should they be employed simultaneously in a true *development* system. Remember the wise advice of Confucius, *"He who chases two rabbits catches neither."*

We will explore the effective use of performance correction and constructive feedback in the workplace, as these techniques are essential to the maintenance of a successful performance management system. As with all things "Human Resources," the key is to remember that there is a time and place, and certainly a correct tone and language, that must be used when engaging in these dialogues.

CHAPTER 2:

Survey Your Top Performers

"It doesn't make sense to hire smart people and tell them what to do;
we hire smart people so they can tell us what to do."

—Steve Jobs

The average employee working today will change jobs as many as seven or eight times over the course of their career. This statistic almost doubles for new graduates, who are projected to make at least 15 job moves throughout their working life.

The cost of turnover to your organization is tremendous. Companies are very good at tracking the cost of wages, benefits, insurance, recruiting and so on, yet most have only a vague concept of what turnover is *truly* costing them, both in terms of actual dollars and in more intangible ways such as reduced productivity, impairments to morale and culture, and lost time due to the on-boarding and training of new staff.

Studies have shown that the actual cost of replacing an employee can be as high as 50-60% of the employee's annual salary, and even as high as 90-200% of their salary once you add in the expenses of recruitment, training your new hire, job errors and/or lost sales, and various other undesirable events and lost productivity that may be caused by having a new person on your team[4].

Of course, some turnover is necessary and even desirable. For example, replacing chronic underperformers with people who have fresh ideas, enthusiasm and expertise is key to the success of your organization. However, the goal is to retain your most valued employees – those people whose skills, knowledge and work ethic would be extremely difficult to replace.

The best way to get inside the mind of your top performers is to conduct an independent engagement survey. Do it now, not after they hand in a resignation letter! Ask them what they enjoy about their job, your culture, reasons why they might leave, and what they need to be more engaged and productive in their work. If people are thinking about leaving, find out what would make them stay. Just the fact that you've shown an interest in their workplace satisfaction can go a long way, but most importantly, you will discover valuable information about improvements you can make that will benefit your organization and your staff as a whole.

Some sample questions may include:

How do you feel about coming in to work each day?

What has your manager/supervisor done recently to inspire you to do a better job?

What are three things you would change about your job if you could?

Give an example of a competitive offer or opportunity that would compel you to leave.

Describe your idea of the perfect job for you.

What do you love most about your job?

Try to keep the line of questioning positive, and always ask open-ended questions that will stimulate conversation, not questions that can be answered with "yes" or "no". You might be surprised by some of the information that comes up. Typically, your best employees are the ones who are least likely to complain, so this type of informal survey is a great way to give them an opportunity to say what is really on their mind.

Some employers choose to conduct anonymous surveys through a third party (more on this in Chapter 12). This will encourage participation and candor from your staff, and is a good way to pinpoint problems that people are not eager to bring out into the open. An anonymous survey is not meant as a replacement for dialogue with your team, but can be used as a tool across all staff and departments to get a general sense of satisfaction levels among people in all areas of your organization.

The main goal of surveying top performers is, of course, to keep them on board, but you should also be using this as a strategic opportunity to pinpoint any current or potential retention issue you may have, and subsequently implement programs to address these gaps. Your program should be tailored to meet the unique needs of your organization. Below are a few popular examples of in-house programming that can be used to help hold on to your most valued team players:

Orientation and On-Boarding: A new employee's perception of a workplace is formed very early on, this is why it is so important to make the most of an incumbent's first few weeks on the job. Use this time as an opportunity to educate the employee on what your organization is all about, and what they can do to fit in and feel like a part of the team. Give them time to settle in and get to know other staff members. Don't, however, oversell the job or gloss over any problems that you are experiencing. They will find out eventually, and may become disillusioned with management if they feel that important information was kept from them. An employee's first impression of an organization is formative and is an important early step towards creating the conditions for long-term satisfaction and engagement.

Career Development: Increasingly, career development opportunities outrank compensation issues. For your employees to remain fully engaged they should have an idea of what their career path within your organization will look like. They will be much more likely to stay with you if they have a vision of how their career goals can be met according to 2, 5 and 10-year timelines. Many employees leave jobs because they feel they have "gone as far as they can go" with a particular organization. By offering career planning options, coaching, strengths assessments, and setting developmental goals with your staff that are realistic but challenging, you can help to chart a map of what their future could potentially look like should they choose to work with you in the long-term.

Work/Life Balance: The employers who are the most successful when it comes to retaining high quality staff seem to be the ones who recognize and validate the need for a balanced approach to work and life outside work. It is not realistic to expect your employees to sacrifice their home life or personal life in order to get their job done. If you do need your staff to work above and beyond their normal hours, perhaps due to a special project or looming deadline, give them ample advanced warning and flexibility to take needed time off at another time. Many employers now offer flex time or the opportunity to telecommute and/or work periodically from home. This isn't appropriate for every employer, but think about ways you can provide a little added flexibility to make life easier for your staff. The greater your need as an organization is for peak performance or time commitment over extended periods, the more willing you need to be to offer autonomy and flexibility in kind.

Socialization: Offer social, team building or group training activities which complement your workplace culture, and provide an opportunity for staff to get to know each other beyond the superficial level of daily job interaction. There is no doubt that employees are much more likely to stay with an organization if they feel that they have positive relationships with their direct reports and with their co-workers. Creating a co-operative and affirmative team atmosphere at work is sometimes as simple as providing the occasional opportunity for people to interact in new ways outside of work routines.

Conduct an Exit Interview: If you are unlucky enough to lose a valued member of your team, use this as an opportunity to dialogue with them about why they want to leave, and what you or your organization could have done differently to have avoided this outcome. Within reason, never be afraid to counter offer or to right a wrong if it means you can maintain talent. The exit interview can shed light on some key factors that might be hindering staff retention. You might get more unfiltered answers if this interview is conducted by a third party. Most often, employees quit because they have found a more attractive career path, or wish to avoid a poor supervisor or difficult peer, or are seeking better hours or a better opportunity elsewhere.

Understanding why employees stay with an organization is just as important as understanding why they decide to leave. Some studies have suggested that the more an employee participates in their workplace culture, and the web of relationships and activities that go with this, the more likely they are to stay with an organization in the long-term[5]. It is these social networks and the feeling that they "belong" at work which can make the difference between staying and leaving. If you want to create or further develop this type of positive workplace culture, start by defining what your culture is or could potentially be, and begin working towards supporting those ideals. If your organization is growing, focus future recruiting initiatives on finding the types of people who would flourish in an environment characterized by rapid change, for example.

The supervisor-employee relationship is another key retention factor that sometimes gets overlooked, often because some employees are reticent to admit that their main reason for leaving is not liking their boss. This is however a very common reason for resignations. Understandably, they don't want to leave on bad terms and possibly jeopardize what might otherwise be a good reference. A Gallup study of one million employed U.S. workers indicates that their number one reason for wanting to leave their current position (or for quitting a job in the past) has been a poor relationship with their manager or direct supervisor[6].

"People leave managers not companies... in the end, turnover is mostly a manager issue," Gallup reported in its survey findings. They also determined that poorly-managed work groups are on average 50 percent less productive and 44 percent less profitable than well-managed groups, and that over 60% of workers were "not engaged". Low engagement levels cost money – this study pegged the cost to North American businesses in the $450 - 550 billion range. That's *billions*, not millions.

Clearly, the need exists for organizations to better prepare managers and supervisors to foster positive and constructive relationships with their direct reports. Not every manager is going to come to the table with the level of interpersonal and leadership skill that is needed to create the "teamwork climate" you want in your workplace. For that reason it is critical that you create an intentional system for professional development that promotes the right environment for growth and engagement, and give your leadership team the tools and resources to support their staff. Regrettably, many organizations focus on "execution", operations and strategic planning, and not enough on developing systematic and effective processes for developing performance through their people. Strategic plans may be critical to your organization's path and its success in its mission, but strat-plans don't build culture and engagement in and of themselves. You need to do more, differently.

CHAPTER 3:

Creating a High Performance Work System

"Great vision without great people is irrelevant."

– Jim Collins

A High Performance Work System (HPWS) can be defined as an interrelated system of HR practices and policies that includes rigorous recruitment and selection processes, performance-contingent incentive compensation, performance management, a commitment to employee involvement, and extensive training & development opportunities. This chapter will outline step-by-step how you can set the table for a HPWS framework that will work in your organization.

Step 1: Setting objectives

Building the foundation of a High Performance Work System must begin with taking a critical look at what objectives you wish to fulfill for your staff. Some questions for you to consider may include:

❖   What do you wish your staff would do more of? Less of? Differently?

❖ Is there anything you could change about your leadership style to create a better relationship with your employees?

❖ What's working well with your current processes? What's not working?

This is a starting point. In Chapter 6, we will discuss best practices for setting high quality objectives that can provide some of the answers to these questions.

Step 2: Recruitment and Selection

If you are building a new business, expanding current operations, or replacing staff, then Recruitment is definitely your most important order of business. The recruitment and selection process is not one where corners can be cut or decisions made in haste. There should be a saying, "Hire in haste, repent at leisure!". Even if you've decided to hire someone recommended by a relative or current employee, make sure you follow a consistent, structured process. Once an employee has been hired, you have made a commitment that is not always so easy to get out of, particularly once the probationary period has passed (and yes, there should always be a probationary period, detailed in your written employment agreement). Though it's clearly a minority, regrettably, not all job applicants are as forthcoming as they should be[7]:

❖ 11% have a criminal record

❖ 90% with criminal records mislead / lie concerning those convictions

❖ 6% supply false Social Insurance numbers

- ❖ 23% have used alternate names / an alias

- ❖ 25% exaggerate the duration of previous employment

- ❖ 20% of applicants have poor references

- ❖ 9% have mislead / lied about their education

- ❖ 12% have bad credit

Even if you are working with a professional recruiter, your organization's own screening process must be rigorous. A structured interview process that includes behavior-based questions and skills assessments is recommended, along with a complete background check, and review of at least three references from previous employers. Ensure that references come from former employers or supervisors, and not only from co-workers or that person's own reporting staff (although these references can provide excellent context as well).

If a candidate is unwilling to ask a former boss to provide a reference, this is a red flag that should not be ignored. Also beware of candidates who have a long list of grievances against former employers. While difficulty with a previous employer is not entirely uncommon, a string of bad experiences can be indicative of something else that requires further discernment. The bottom line is this: it is not enough for a person to have an impressive resume or dazzle you in an interview – if you have any uncertainty during the recruitment process, and certainly if any concerns come up during a reference or background check, it may be best to keep looking.

Don't cut corners with people selection. Even if you have the budget to fund significant training and professional development opportunities, these resources will not address a fundamental mismatch between your requirements and a candidate's core competencies. Define what you need as precisely as possible and then find that person.

Step 3: Performance Contingent Incentive Compensation

We've said that employee performance is not totally driven by compensation, and it isn't, but one's pay cheque is still a pretty important reason for many of us going in to work every day. Having a tangible means of rewarding performance can produce results if reward systems are properly aligned with performance outcomes and deliverables. There is nothing wrong with this form of "reward for work" system, as long as it is used in tandem with the other performance strategies and not as a sole means of motivation. A few pointers for your financial incentive program include:

❖ Do your research to ascertain whether your incentive program (and compensation levels in general) are market competitive and appropriate for your industry or organization. Remember that incentives are not just cash - they could be time-off provisions, benefits, retirement savings, training opportunities, wellness packages, bonuses (the list goes on!). As we will continue to discover, motivation is complex and there is no 'magic bullet' approach that will individually engage every employee, every time.

❖ Make sure you have detailed, in writing, the goals or outcomes that must be achieved for the incentive to apply. There cannot be any room for interpretation with this – there must be a strategy that is specific and clearly communicated in place to ensure your incentive program engages and remains fair across all employees and departments.

❖ While having a clearly understood program is key, you do not need to have a "one-size-fits-all" program for every employee. Depending on the size of your organization and the type of business you are in, your program may be tailored differently to suit the unique contributions of certain employees or departments. What is most important is that employees in similar situations with similar accountabilities are able to take advantage of the same incentives.

❖ Balance Team Results and Individual Goals: If compensation is based on overall results, employees will behave differently than they will if compensation is based on individual results. If team performance is critical, ensure compensation recognizes and rewards team behavior. If individual achievements are important, push these levers. Carefully balancing individual and team goals with incentives is essential, and will help you avoid misfires.

❖ When it comes to incentive "payouts," perception is all-important. There cannot be any perception among your staff that there has been unfair recognition to favored employees, or that the deserving have been under-compensated. Employees need to know that their performance has been measured objectively against a pre-determined standard – not according to the whims of a supervisor. It all goes back to having a concrete incentive strategy and sticking to it.

❖ If you are relying on cash rewards, don't try to simplify a bonus program by rolling the funds into base pay – this might be a time saver but rather defeats the purpose, creating an entitlement mentality where employees expect a bonus as a standard part of their compensation.

Most of these strategies speak to extrinsic ('cash') rewards. Quantifiable recognition is the easy part. In fact, many of you don't have unlimited resources and are not in a position to turn on the financial taps to keep everyone humming. As we will see in our Chapter 7 (Motivation) it's not that easy. Sustainable, profound engagement requires additional planning and a systems approach to developing individual commitment.

Step 4: Performance Management

As earlier discussed, an effective Performance Management System has two distinct but supporting channels of operation. The first, focussed on Performance Development strategies, is independent of its inverse image, Performance Correction.

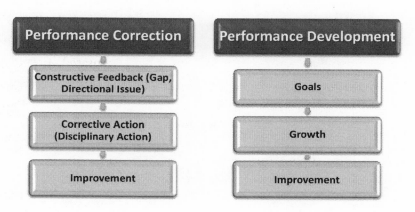

We repeat this distinction throughout this work as it is foundational. It is critical that you get it right and decide which side of the highway you're going to be driving on before you initiate a discussion with an employee.

When employed at the right time, in the right way, Performance Correction has just as important a place in your Performance Management Program as Performance Development. Both operational systems support healthy working relationships and an effective workplace culture. Some considerations when developing corrective strategies include:

❖ *Use "Root Cause Analysis" to identify Performance Issues.* Before you focus on what an employee has done "wrong", find out the reason why this incident or behavior has occurred in the first place. Aim your performance improvement strategy at the root cause, rather than merely treating the symptom of the problem (more on this in Chapter 5).

❖ *Distinguish between Subjective & Objective Assessments.* Only deal in information that is supported by direct observation or verifiable facts. The personal opinion of fellow co-workers or managers is not going to give you an accurate picture of events – stick to the facts at all times! (More on this in Chapter 6).

❖ *Set Effective Performance Objectives and Goals.* Undesirable behavior can be changed if you communicate the behavior desired. Goal setting is a good place to start. Objectives need to be specific, measurable, and should always include a deadline, outcome or target for review. Focus on targets that will modify, improve or redirect employee behavior, while still remaining realistic and achievable (more on this in Chapter 7).

❖ *Deliver Effective & Constructive Feedback.* Effective feedback can support performance correction. At times, constructive feedback must also be considered to realign performance. In this case, focus on the conduct or issue, **not** the person. Be very specific about your concerns, and have a constructive purpose for the feedback you are giving. It is important that you have specific suggestions for improvement (more on this in Chapter 8).

❖ *Conduct an effective Performance Discussion.* This is not a forum for criticism. Use feedback as an opportunity to dialogue about concrete performance issues and to collaborate on setting the right path to move forward (more on this in Chapter 9).

Step 5: A Commitment to Employee Involvement

High levels of employee involvement are key to success. A quick review of the "100 Top Companies To Work For" (*in Fortune Magazine – though there are many such 'lists' these days*) shows a not-surprising list of companies that are frequently touted in the media for offering a superior workplace culture. While your business may not be in a position to offer some of the perks available at Google or Microsoft, any employer can show a commitment to their staff by creating a welcoming and inclusive workplace environment. This has less to do with providing coffee bars and private gyms (although if you have the budget for that, great!) and everything to do with actively involving your employees in decision making on an ongoing basis, providing them with appropriate autonomy, and recognizing success. Not only will these efforts keep your staff fully engaged, they will benefit your organization by generating a constant stream of fresh ideas and varied perspectives.

Step 6: Training and Development

If you are thinking you can't spare the resources or hours to offer your employees additional training, you may be missing out on one of the most critical and proven methods of employee engagement out there.

It is a mistake to fail to invest in training and development – studies have shown time and time again that employees who partake in on-the-job training and development initiatives are more effective, more productive, and have a better understanding of their job function and their role within their organization. While this does involve an upfront output of time and money on your part, the benefits outweigh any short-term inconveniences: Improved efficiency and productivity; lower levels of employee turnover and absenteeism; and less supervision required, which frees time for your frontline managers to engage in higher value-added activities, such as leading rather than managing.

Perhaps most significant of all, you will be creating a reserve of resilient, cross-trained employees who can bridge gaps during sudden changes to your organizational structure. Instead of looking at what it may cost you to train and develop your staff, consider the real costs of not doing so.

Creating a HPWS is not easy, nor is it an overnight exercise. Instead of looking for a turnkey solution, get started by focussing on one or two areas. Start with the ones that are most accessible and achievable to support your success. Consider getting some help with the steeper inclines and you will gradually build strength and capability into your organization.

Chapter 4:

Using Root Cause Analysis to Identify Performance Issues

"The difference between a Master and a Beginner: A Master has failed many more times than a Beginner has tried."

–Plato

Root Cause Analysis (RCA) has been a staple of manufacturing and engineering theories for decades as a means of troubleshooting problems by identifying and correcting the root cause of events, as opposed to simply addressing their symptoms. While RCA has been proven to help manage safety, quality, maintenance, and production issues, it can also be highly effective when it comes to dealing with people and performance challenges.

Although a fairly simplistic distillation of Root Cause theories, the following are six basic steps that we recommend you should consider before addressing performance issues and setting goals:

1.   Define the problem or performance gap

2. Gather data and evidence (objectively!)

3. Ask "why": Identify all relationships associated with the problem

4. Identify whether the causes (if removed or changed) would prevent a recurrence

5. Identify solutions that would prevent a recurrence, are within your control, *and* meet your goals – *without* causing other problems

6. Implement solutions collaboratively (ask employees to suggest options for improvement - it's their career, not yours).

To be effective, RCA must be performed systematically and backed up by documented evidence. Also keep in mind that there is often more than one root cause for a given problem.

Central to RCA is the "5 Why" Analysis – a system which allows you to investigate an issue from all angles to ensure that as many contributors as possible are reviewed and addressed up front. This makes it possible to create an action plan taking into account all the information, up to and including the "Root Cause." Toddlers intuitively ask "why" on a regular basis to discover information and to orient themselves to situations they have not yet encountered. We lose this innocence through socialization but it is an instinct we should reacquaint ourselves with to evaluate and manage issues at work and in our personal lives.

A sample "5 Why" Analysis

Ted didn't get to work on time. He has been late almost every day for the past two weeks! Here is the dialogue which occurred between Ted and his Supervisor:

Supervisor: Ted, why were you late again this morning?

Ted: My car wouldn't start.

Supervisor: Why wouldn't the car start?

Ted: The lights were left on again.

Supervisor: Why were the lights on?

Ted: The kids have been playing in the car after dinner.

Supervisor: Why have you been letting your kids play in your car?

Ted: I've been leaving them with a babysitter some evenings so I can get caught up on work in my home-office.

So, it turns out there are two issues here: Ted has too much work to complete during regular office hours, and he needs a new babysitter. The latter problem is up to Ted to solve, but the former is an HR and perhaps structural matter which needs to be addressed before Ted burns out. Though this is a trivial example, it highlights the necessity of questioning the root cause of an issue before arriving at a conclusion.

While RCA can be used to pinpoint and troubleshoot specific employee issues, it can also be used on a larger scale to identify organizational problems such as the inability to attract the "right talent," high staff turnover, or the insidious spread of low morale.

For RCA to be effective in this context you have to step back to basics and re-introduce yourself to what your business or organization is all about. Conduct interviews with key people to get a sense of the less obvious factors that may be contributing to your current circumstances. Ask questions such as:

❖ What is our management and leadership style?

❖ How has our financial performance evolved over the past several years?

❖ What are the best words to describe our organizational culture?

❖ What have we done differently this year, compared with last year?

❖ Have there been staff issues that were not adequately addressed?

❖ Are there any common patterns we have noticed with staff behavior?

❖ Are there external market influences at play that could be causing a shift?

Whatever answers you come up with, you need to keep asking why, why, why? Work with your team to brainstorm some hypotheses. Do not exclude or discount any possible theories or explanations at this point. Get everything on the table. The more data you can collect to help determine causal factors, the better.

This sounds like a time consuming endeavour, but it doesn't have to be. At a minimum, your RCA session could take the form of a team building exercise that will create some food for thought among your staff. On a grander scale, it might help you rethink the way you and your senior team are handling human resources and organizational initiatives. When implemented into strategic planning and applied systematically, RCA has the potential to transform an old culture that reacts to problems into a new culture that troubleshoots and resolves issues before they escalate.

CHAPTER 5:

Distinguishing Between Subjective and Objective Assessments

"Objective Reality and Truth requires neither ones consent nor dissent."
– R. Alan Woods

Everyone has bias. As soon as you make an assessment of any person or situation, you have the potential for bias. Unfortunately, not every job can be exclusively measured according to tangible factors such as sales targets or "number of units produced per hour." When measuring workplace outcomes such as customer service, teamwork, reliability, or professionalism, you may be relying largely on your own opinion or the opinion of others. The best way to avoid subjective bias is to ground your views in direct observations, facts, dialogue and on-going assessment.

It is critical to understand the Subjective-Objective dichotomy and to ensure that all aspects of your performance management system are positively grounded in objective criteria. While this sounds elementary, it is a fundamental building block that too often gets glossed over. As an illustration, let's look at the following subjective statement:

"At these levels, the stock market represents an excellent investment opportunity."

That's clearly a matter of opinion and therefore subjective. Of course, we could marshal statistical evidence, trend data and other informed sources to support this view and establish an objective basis for what is otherwise a subjective view - but at face value, it is simply an opinion. An objective assessment of the stock market would be represented as:

"The TSX closed yesterday at 14,590, up 100 points from the market's previous close."

Of course, neatly organizing employee performance data into one category or other isn't always possible or even desirable. What is important is that your baseline orientation when providing feedback or conducting a development discussion be firmly in the objective camp, not the subjective. This is basic "HR Hygiene" and the essential foundation that your performance system will be built upon, so it is critical that you get it right.

It is no doubt easier to be objective when talking about stock market data than it is when talking about people. It is even more difficult when you are dealing with an employee whose performance you are not particularly happy with. Keep in mind that being "objective" doesn't mean you can't get your point across. It is more about using the right language to create a dialogue that is based on fact, not on personality or opinion.

Below are some examples of how you can remove a subjective tone from your employee discourse:

Subjective: *"Judy, your work is just not up to par with the work of the other office clerks. You're always behind schedule turning in projects and you need to upgrade your computer skills."*

Objective: *"Judy, let's review some recent work you completed. I see here that you were five days late handing in the report on the Dominion Project, and that your Excel charts for Accounting had several mistakes in them. In July, and again in September, we asked you to sign up for an advanced Excel course, and we don't have any record of this being completed. What can we do to fix this situation?"*

Subjective: *"Al, you're always late, I'm tired of hearing excuses!"*

Objective: *"Al, according to your attendance record, you have been late six times in the past month. On one occasion you missed the first half of a very important meeting involving a new client. We need to address this."*

Subjective: *"Ron, you're just not dealing well with the customers – people find you very aggressive and you really need to work on your communication skills or else we'll have to move you to another department."*

Objective: *"Ron, you engaged in an argument with a customer on January 4th, and then on February 2nd another customer indicated that you were rude to them. I want to ensure we better manage our relationships with customers. What can you do to make sure this doesn't happen again?"*

As you can see, we've not only shifted the focus from personality to behavior, we have provided concrete examples of events that have been documented. Either an event occurred or it did not – this is an objective fact. The reason for the event occurring is up to the employee to explain, and they should be given this opportunity, regardless of how much in the wrong you *personally* feel they might be.

Other bias pitfalls to avoid when evaluating employee performance include:

Lack of Differentiation: Managers can have a tendency to avoid controversy when conducting the evaluations of their direct reports and as a consequence they may evaluate all employees similarly. One of the solutions to this problem formed part of the "rank-and-yank" strategy Jack Welch implemented during his remarkable career as the CEO of General Electric. He required all managers to evaluate their direct reports on a comparative and relative basis. Therefore, if a Manager had 10 employees - no matter how similar their levels of performance might be - he required that they rank them in order from 1 through 10 to effectively eliminate differentiation issues. Many have followed the GE model including Microsoft during Steve Ballmer's leadership. Microsoft's version called "stack ranking" proved ineffective, and counterproductive: In fact, top performers quickly avoided working with other high-performing peers for fear of being compared to this relatively high standard. While forced ranking minimizes the tendency to rank everyone similarly, unfortunately it also promotes dissension and undermines teamwork – an increasingly essential requirement for organizational effectiveness. So be mindful of the lack-of-differentiation tendency but at the same time, do not adopt an overly simplistic ranking strategy.

Recency Effect: This occurs when a Manager weighs an employee's recent performance (good or bad) too heavily rather than looking at the entire evaluation period. So if an employee had an outstanding year overall but made a critical error in the week that preceded their performance evaluation, the Recency Effect would lead to that evaluation disproportionately considering the more recent error rather than looking at the solid track record of the entire year.

Personal Bias: As it suggests, this is an often subconscious tendency to lend more generous performance feedback to employees who share things in common with the evaluating Manager (age, race, gender, interests etc). We must be mindful of this tendency when assessing others who may be (very) different from ourselves.

Halo Effect: The Halo Effect is a subtle subjective influence. It occurs when a manager associates an employee's strengths in certain areas (often ones very important to the organization) as indicative of the employee's overall performance - or worse still, causes the manager to overlook deficiencies in other areas given the employee's strong delivery on the things important to the manager or organization. A manager must avoid this tendency to translate a high level of competency or performance in a specific area as an automatic indication of exceptional general performance or exceptional performance in a number of unrelated areas.

All of these subjective influences must be carefully monitored and eliminated in your quest to organize an effective review of performance.

Organizing your Data

What should you look at to assess performance? Objective, factual information and assessments grounded in this data. A simple method borrowed from the world of academics, and used by many school boards across North America, is called the *Triangulation of Assessment*. Triangulation is an overarching assessment strategy that uses different methods, such as performance data and multi-source feedback, to collect assessment data over a period of time.

A workplace Triangulation Assessment might look something like this:

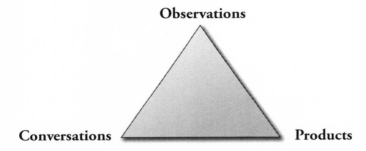

Observations are simply that, direct review of actual work performance. Observations can occur at any time and allow the person making the assessment to observe the employee in any capacity: for example, working with others (customers, peers) or working with different concepts. This process allows the collection and tracking of information in an effective and accurate manner.

Conversations: If you're not having a regular dialogue with your staff, you need to. Not only is this an invaluable and primary source of assessment information, it is an essential tool for engaging employees and ensuring they remain informed and aligned with organizational direction and priorities. It also builds rapport and is essential to developing relationships. Relationships - not just superficial contact - are essential

40

to building trust and engagement in your culture. Conversations with other interested participants (co-workers, customers) can also enlarge the information available for assessment, but ensure you maintain an objective focus (avoid uncorroborated "hearsay," for example).

Products are tangible materials or outcomes created by the employee (widgets, tasks or projects). These outputs can then be compared (triangulated) with the discoveries found in Conversations and Observations.

All three sources of information allow Manager and Employee to engage in a dialogue about performance and how it can be developed, from an objective foundation. Triangulation is an excellent model to both collect information and to then compare and qualify the data received against each other. While it is perfectly acceptable to apply information collected from only one point of the triangle, it will be more reliable if you can verify its accuracy using the other two points of contact.

The following is a simple example of how Triangulation could be applied in a small business setting:

John owns a landscaping company that is hired by a family who wants an interlocking brick walkway installed at their front entrance. John delegates this job to Rick, who designs three possible plans for the homeowners to choose from. They approve one of the designs and Risk proceeds to requisition materials and schedule a crew to complete the project.

John doesn't use an annual performance development appraisal with his staff, but instead uses a project review and feedback system to discuss performance in real time. Before the crew is dispatched and the materials are ordered, John reviews and approves the site plan and materials requisition prepared by Rick (Observation). After the project is installed at the customer's home, John stops in to inspect the site for structural integrity, aesthetic finish, and to ensure the location has been properly cleaned up (Work Product). Finally, if the homeowners are not available when John completes his site inspection, he initiates a follow-up call to ensure that they are completely satisfied and to determine any further corrections or follow up that might be required (Conversation).

Presenting Your Data

Remaining grounded in objective territory is not just about dealing in facts, it also has to do with the manner by which you address the other person. Use non-judgmental language and an even tone of voice that does not indicate emotional reaction, impatience or frustration. You do not want to convey the message that you are letting emotions (subjective!) affect your decision making process, which should of course always be based on the facts, and not on whether or not you or other people in your organization dislike a certain employee. Of course, you don't want to be so "hygienic" that you appear disinterested. Be genuine.

Use all three corners of the triangle to ensure you have objective data on file. It is an invaluable resource for a development plan – and on the other end of the performance management spectrum – in the event you need to address a performance gap. If a difficult situation should arise, you need to be able to go to the individual's employee file and find a complete record of events which have occurred, and the dates they occurred on. You don't want to be in a situation where you have to rely on hearsay and undocumented personal recollection. More important than that, everyone (especially your staff) should know where they stand. If there are performance issues, they should be clearly communicated so that your staff have an opportunity to address concerns. A healthy relationship requires candor and transparency, especially when a difficult conversation is needed.

To be objective, you need data, and for there to be data, you need to maintain complete employee records for every individual on your team. You may think a matter is too trivial to bother making a formal record of it, but sometimes what seems like an innocuous event in the moment later snowballs into a large-scale issue. Employee A and Employee B got into a disagreement over who was supposed to write the report. The matter seemed to be settled, but two months later Employee A files a harassment complaint against Employee B. Does anyone remember what their argument was about back in December? Did it even happen in December? Have there been other conflicts between the two parties that were never reported?

Ultimately, keeping detailed records of incidents which occur in your workplace (both good and bad) is not just a solid HR practice, it allows for the creation of a store of data that will become the groundwork of your performance management system. For this system to work, you must be dealing in verifiable fact and documented events. This is true even if you are dealing with the best employee in the world. What has that person done in the past year to merit this status? Your comments can never be based on personality or on "liking" someone. There can't be the perception among your staff that they are in some sort of popularity contest – this will create hard feelings, guaranteed! Feedback must be based on events and actions which have occurred, not on any personal opinion you may have.

This information is not only valuable to an employer. Employees have an equal, perhaps greater, interest in ensuring there is accurate information available concerning their job performance and career aspirations. An effective performance development system (as we will later discuss) is forward-thinking and will establish a roadmap for success by creating a formalized approach to career development. This is achieved by identifying resources and critical experiences, and scaffolding goals to achieve professional and career objectives.

Though perhaps not as progressively oriented, a documented track-record which speaks to a person's achievements and contributions is something every employee should be vitally interested in seeing in their "file." If a new manager comes on the scene, where is the institutional memory of everything the employee has achieved? In the event a new manager concludes the employee is no longer a fit, there should be some baseline information which either supports or contradicts this assessment. This is a cynical perspective but it illustrates the vested interest employees must have in the process -- the more noble goals of development and self-actualization will override in a well managed system.

CHAPTER 6:

Setting High-Quality Performance Objectives

"Never discourage anyone who continually makes progress,
no matter how slow."

– Plato

How do you earn loyalty from your staff? If you're fortunate enough to employ a chaplain or any other type of religious figure as a part of your organization (which may be the case if you run a school or hospital, as an example), you're already blessed with Polity: The institutionalized philosophy that a priest's mission in the church is to support the ongoing integrity and stability of their "employer," sometimes at the expense of not being in a position to fully pursue personal or professional interests. While you may never achieve polity in your business, we can learn much from religious ministries about how to galvanize organizational culture and drive engagement.

Put aside for a moment your perspectives on religion. While ecclesiastical communities have their own challenges, they are characterized by high levels of personal commitment and ministers who often put their vocational callings ahead of their personal needs in the interest of advancing the ideology of their faith and the maintenance of the institution itself. Of course, there are many fundamental drivers (outside the scope of this work), not the least of which is the unique calling of those who pursue a role in the church.

Faith systems are also highly aligned with goal attainment and the visualization of those objectives. To wit, the 10 Commandments. There are many other organizational characteristics that support the powerful cultural identity and engagement within religious communities (whether it be a church, a mosque, a synagogue, a temple or another faith-based community), but let's further develop the concept of powerful goal-setting such as those embraced in religious communities. Motivational objectives play a pivotal role in creating an effective performance development system, and are a key part of the journey to realize *polity* in our organizations and cultures.

It is a fact that goal-setting influences behavior. People work harder to achieve difficult goals. Challenging, but still attainable, goals will influence behavior and drive motivation in a positive direction.

Renowned business author Daniel Pink[8] defines this as the "Goldilocks Principle": Namely, setting goals which are neither too difficult nor too easy to achieve. In his motivation theory, Pink uses the term "Goldilocks tasks" to describe those tasks which will push employees out of their comfort zones, allowing them to stretch themselves and develop their competencies further. Giving an employee responsibilities that are too simplified for their skill level will result in boredom, but if the goals you set are too challenging, employees might become frustrated, overwhelmed or stressed. The key is to find a balance in goal-setting where the employee is at the maximum end of their ability scale without being pushed beyond it.

Ultimately, people will work harder when they are presented with more difficult goals. If you are not setting challenging but attainable goals for your employees, they will have nothing to work towards, nor will they have a clear definition of your expectations.

A Goal or Objective should:

❖ Be Specific, Measurable, and should include a Deadline, Outcome or Target (a "DOT") for review.

❖ Focus on targets that will stretch Employee Performance.

❖ Not simply be a description or listing of tasks.

❖ Produce meaningful results.

Defining clear performance objectives helps to ensure that every member of your team knows what is expected of them and what the end results should be. This needs to be done in writing, and should be readily accessible to all parties. Goals which are documented in writing are more likely to be achieved. Whether you decide to develop this documentation on your own or with outside help, there are some basic steps that can be followed to help ensure that your employees remain engaged in this process:

Think about results: You should always have in mind what you hope the end result to be. Whether this is a sales target or an upgrading of a software skill, be clear about what the ultimate expectation is for the employee. Wherever possible we encourage you to focus on *results* and avoid the tendency to (micro) manage the steps involved in achieving the outcome. Provided the employee's method for producing what you want to see doesn't violate some legal, moral or cultural norm in your organization, give them the latitude and autonomy to achieve that success by leveraging the best of their talents.

Make sure it's Achievable: Objectives must be realistic and achievable – the purpose is to motivate your employees to succeed, not to set them up for a downfall. We like to say that you should "DOT" all of your goals (which means you should establish a Deadline, Outcome or Target for all goals).

Put objectives in the context of larger organizational goals: One of the best ways to spark motivation is to help employees feel like they are part of a bigger picture, and that their contribution, however small, has an impact on the overall growth and wellbeing of your organization. Look for specific examples of how the achievement of their objectives will impact the success of the organization. Make sure you've already clearly established your own goals and those of the organization at the strategic level. If you have not already done this, you will find that setting goals at a team and individual level will be very difficult and will produce a patchwork approach to goal setting rather than a clearly aligned mission throughout your organization.

How will the end result be measured? Once the goal has been determined, the employee needs to know how their achievement of this goal will be measured. Specify whether they will need to complete a certification, provide sales spreadsheets, make a presentation, or provide some other form of completion or success to show that their objective has been met and understood. Better still, involve them in this discussion to increase the probability of success and true ownership.

It is worth repeating, make sure you're focused on results and outcomes: Many companies evaluate employee performance based on effort and number of tasks, not results or value. Extra effort and commitment to task should matter, but make sure you're not strictly recognizing "busy work" alone. Results and outcomes represent value, and your performance measurement systems need to prioritize and reward those achievements, not just worker-bee activity.

Create clear timelines: Ideally there should be a definitive start and end date established for each goal. Otherwise objectives tend to get lost in the shuffle of competing priorities.

Many of us are familiar with the SMART methodology for goal-setting (making objectives Specific, Measurable, Achievable, Realistic and Time-bound). It's a great technique (and a clever acronym), so try applying this to all of your goal-setting initiatives. We simplify the rules for goal-setting further into three clear steps as follows:

Identify the Performance Objective (Goal or Target)

1

Agree on a Measurement Criteria

Establish a Deadline, Outcome or Target (DOT) for Review

Specific, quantifiable and challenging (attainable) goals motivate effort and drive performance. Other goal setting best practices to consider include:

❖ **Clarity:** Make sure goals are absolutely clear and communicated.

❖ **Empower:** Once Objectives have been clearly defined/ communicated, empower people to do their work.

❖ **Focus:** Focus on one, two or three meaningful goals at a time. Doing more than this dilutes focus and the likelihood of success. Moreover, if you are including six or seven goals in a performance process it is quite likely that you are simply restating some of the key objectives or tasks associated with the person's job description rather than setting true stretch targets for development.

❖ Think "Goldilocks"

❖ Ensure all of your Goals have a DOT (**D**eadline, **O**utcome or **T**arget for review).

With that said, the most important consideration in any goal-setting exercise is to involve the employee. Their participation, and ideally sponsorship, in setting objectives is a critical pre-cursor to ensuring ownership for the goal and a motivated approach to its achievement. This is not to say you shouldn't implement broad strategic goals across your organization that apply to all employees. You should.

Leaders should lead, but just keep in mind that employee input into larger-scale strategic planning will increase the likelihood that individual behavior will line up with organizational direction. It will also support the "operationalizing" of those strategic directives amongst your team to ensure they are actually executed and don't simply remain on a decorative mission statement in your lobby.

At a day-to-day level of organizational function, it is clear that unilateral goal-setting without collaboration and staff input will diminish the probability that objectives will be achieved. This remains true even if these objectives are linked to incentives and other extrinsic rewards.

Let's apply these techniques to a case study to practice their implications:

❖ Carl is the newest employee in a medium-sized medical devices manufacturer owned by a local family. He is a recent graduate of a community college Life Sciences program, and was hired on the recommendation of one of the owner's children who played competitive-level hockey with Carl during their time together in high school.

❖ Carl performs work to an acceptable level, only. He is cooperative with co-workers and produces reasonable work, usually with some minor errors. Work is most often, but not always, finished on time – but just in time, consistently at the "11th hour".

❖ Carl does the minimum required, showing no extra effort or commitment to his work, or his own development as an employee.

❖ Develop a goal-based performance plan to discuss with Carl.

Try practicing some of your Objective-setting skills based on this Case Study (have a go at providing Feedback too, a topic we will cover in the following chapters). A Performance Plan has also been provided in the Appendices that maps out suggested solutions and approaches for dealing with these issues constructively with Carl.

GE Knew About this 50 Years Ago...

The seminal work of three General Electric industrial psychologists 50 years ago confirms the effectiveness of these goal-setting strategies. It was ground breaking in its day, but many organizations have yet to embrace these fundamental tenets in their performance systems over half a century later. In a nutshell, the personnel management team (as it was then known) at GE (Herbert Meyer, Emanuel Kay & John R.P. French Jr.) who published their work in the Harvard Business Journal[9] recommended that the following considerations be embedded in objective-setting and effective performance development systems:

- Employee participation in Goal-setting improves its effectiveness

- Performance improves when specific Goals are established

- Criticism has no positive motivational effect on individual performance

- Collaborative, continuing goal-setting, not criticism, improves performance

- Coaching should be a day-to-day, not a once-a-year, activity

- Appraisals should not be simultaneously held with salary or promotion discussions (Intrinsic Motivation).

Simple, right? While these principles will provide sound governance for any system of development, honestly reflect on your own employee appraisal program: Does it address and take into account these core concepts?

The final conclusion in their study was controversial in its time and still challenges many organizational conventions today. Namely, the advice that performance appraisals and compensation decisions should *not* be automatically linked to one another. On its face, that doesn't line up with the logical argument that pay should follow performance. After all, that is the mantra that drives most performance and compensation policies - policies that have been cemented into organizational practices in lock-step fashion for decades, if not centuries.

Instead, the GE paper recognized the superficial connection between extrinsic rewards (pay raises, bonuses) and employee motivation, but concluded that deeper development and profound engagement could only be fully realized with less tangible, intrinsic engagement techniques. Why else, the author stated, did people volunteer their time to charitable causes, sit on not-for-profit boards and so on. These deeper and self propelling *intrinsic* drivers motivated and sustained commitment in a way that cash cannot - not at least without regular, increasing levels of funding to reinforce continued performance.

It was for these reasons that their paper concluded, and we recommend, that you do not robotically tie your development system to the fortunes of your salary budget - not at least if you want to foster development beyond a perfunctory level. To do otherwise is to run the risk of having your employees (and managers) run rough-shod over your development program to get to the finish line, to see what they will "get." Worse still, your system becomes positioned as a bargaining tool that determines compensation. In this type of work culture, staff will take positions to ensure maximum participation in compensation awards. That is a predictable outcome and one that will significantly undermine the potential growth opportunities in your development system. It will also guarantee that a steady reliance on extrinsic cash rewards will be required to drive daily performance.

Mounting evidence on the workplace psychology front continues to suggest that, in certain circumstances, getting paid more may make you more likely to *dislike* your job. Psychologists call this "cognitive dissonance" -- people will evaluate the pleasure they receive from an activity as lower when they are rewarded with material goods like money because it makes the activity seem unpleasant. The more unpleasant the task, the greater the financial incentive required to compensate for the indignity of completing it (so to speak). In other words, the presence of a salary creates a negative motivation, which makes people like the work less than if they were to do it for free. However, don't take this to the extreme! Completely eliminating (or suppressing) cash rewards will also have a predictable impact on motivation. As we are about to discuss, Maslow's Needs Theory reminds us that you must still meet the basic sustenance needs of your employees in order to move on to higher levels of engagement and satisfaction. No one said managing performance was easy or without real and apparent contradictions. Striking the optimal balance is as much art as science.

When it comes to motivation, we suggest that you take the higher road and tap into the more sustainable stream of intrinsic motivation that is most readily accessed when you appeal to an individual's development and engagement drivers at a genuine level, without the additional distraction of compensation decisions. This renewable motivation resource, popularized and expertly surveyed in Pink's work, will deliver results but you must first abandon the traditional chain-link between professional development and compensation programs.

Chapter 7:

Motivation

"If you can hire people whose passion intersects with the job, they won't require any supervision at all. They will manage themselves better than anyone could ever manage them. Their fire comes from within, not from without. Their motivation is internal, not external."
– Stephen Covey, Author The Seven Habits of Highly Effective People

Before we go further, we need to talk about motivation.

Motivation may be most simply defined as the set of drivers that causes people to act in certain ways. The goal of a manager is to encourage desirable behaviors and to intervene and take corrective actions to curb conduct that is undesirable. An individual's performance in the workplace is a function of their ability to do the job, the resources available to do their job, and their motivation or desire to do the job. An economist might be tempted to illustrate this simple performance definition with the following formula:

Performance = function (Ability × Resources × Motivation)

Several motivational theorists have provided a number of models to explain individual motivation, together with ideas to better exploit potential. While this is not a central objective of this book, and others have done a far better job comparing and analyzing the different perspectives that abound, it is useful to review the theoretical platforms in any attempt to discover and improve upon systems for managing and developing performance in the workplace.

One of the most widely discussed and versatile motivational theories is Abraham Maslow's *Hierarchy of Needs*. Maslow spent a good deal of his career investigating how people could achieve what he termed 'self-actualization'. Essentially how we each go about realizing our true potential. He theorized that the achievement of higher order "self-actualization" was only possible after more basic physiological needs were satisfied. In rank order of needs, his five-stage model is as follows:

1. Basic Biological and Physiological needs: Air, food, drink, shelter, warmth, sleep.

2. Safety needs: Security, order, law, limits, stability, freedom from fear, protection from the elements.

3. Social needs: Belonging, affection and love, peers, family, friends, romantic relationships.

4. Esteem needs: Achievement, mastery, independence, status, dominance, prestige, self-respect, respect from others.

5. Self-Actualization needs: Realizing personal potential, self-fulfillment, seeking personal growth and fulfillment.

To apply this theory to the workplace, the following diagram represents a pyramid of need that must be fulfilled in order for an employee to feel fully self-actualized in their work:

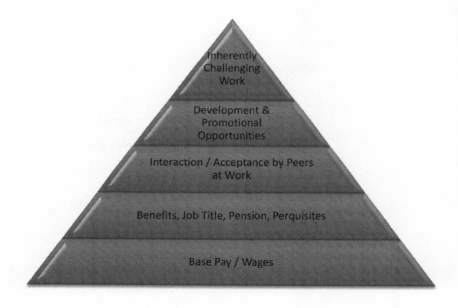

Even the most skilful motivational strategist will be unable to lever employee potential if basic needs are not being met. If you're not paying your staff competitively or if they are constantly anxious about their job security, don't expect to foster an environment of self-actualized utopia. Their basic needs are not being met, and they need to be before you can advance to the next level of motivational development in your organization.

With that said, paying competitively and addressing the basic needs of your employees only gets you in the game. Tapping into the rich vein of intrinsic motivation and developing your staff's true potential will require more than simply priming these basic drivers with a steady paycheque and a plan for tomorrow, as we will discover throughout this book.

A second theory recommended for consideration is the "two factor theory" offered by American Psychologist, Frederick Herzberg[11]. Herzberg suggests that employee job satisfaction is influenced by two sets of independent factors, which he labeled as Motivators and "Hygiene" factors.

He defined Motivational factors as those that were capable of driving and advancing employee satisfaction, such as achievement, recognition, the intrinsic value of work, accountability and professional growth. Herzberg suggested that only these drivers could promote employee job satisfaction in a positive direction. By contrast, Hygiene factors were those that either led to no satisfaction, or an unfortunate slide into dissatisfaction for the employee experience.

Under this Two-Factor theory, Hygiene factors included working conditions, wages, company policies, and, unfortunately, one's interaction with their supervisor. Herzberg theorized that these factors could not move the needle to the right when it came to individual motivation but instead could at best lead to a neutral motivational experience for the employee. Not an encouraging edict if you are a supervisor or manager in an organization: Under his theory, at best you add nothing to the motivational potential of your workers and worse still, your vain attempts at leadership could undermine motivational achievements.

Two-Factor theory builds upon the underpinnings of Maslow's Hierarchy, and supports the more modern and engaging analysis of Daniel Pink's *Drive*, which suggests that tapping into an individual's intrinsic motivation is the only sustainable way to ensure a positive motivational trajectory, and that extrinsic rewards have only a temporary, "non-renewable" impact on engagement. The dark limitations which the Two-Factor theory imposes on supervisory influence, however, is less compelling and we will demonstrate how the use of effective leadership practices can ensure you are a motivational *agent* rather than a motivation blocker.

A final theory offered for consideration is Expectancy Theory. Simply put, people will be more satisfied if the rewards for their performance result in equitable and fair treatment, not only individually, but vis-à-vis their peers. In fact, in almost every workplace situation, staff are constantly making relative assessments of the rewards and recognition that their efforts attract in comparison to those received by their coworkers. This is simply human nature.

When employees believe they are being equitably rewarded in comparison with their coworkers, they tend to maintain performance based on this balance. Where balance does not exist, efforts will be made to reduce the perceived inequity. This can be achieved a number of ways depending on the disequilibrium being experienced.

If a worker perceives that they are being *overcompensated* (this rarely happens!), they will either increase work produced to justify the rewards, or decrease their work effort with the expectation that compensation will be commensurately adjusted. Alternatively, those who have a penchant for social justice might engage in not always constructive efforts to help their co-workers achieve these superior rewards also.

A more likely perceived imbalance is the employee who believes they are not being adequately compensated. In this situation, one of three things is likely to occur:

1. The employee will slack off;

2. They will request increased compensation; or

3. Failing successful achievement of either of the above, they will simply quit.

This is far from a complete and critical review of all of the possible motivational theories that one could consider as context for positioning their performance development system. There are many complexities wound up in personal motivation. Still, it is a worthwhile exercise to reflect upon how you can influence the motivation of your staff, since this is a completely variable component in the employee performance equation that we stated earlier:

Performance = f (Ability × Resources × Motivation)

Going back to review that formula critically, it becomes clear that of the three factors [Ability, Resources, Motivation] *Motivation* stands out as the one factor which is highly and instantly variable.

An employee's Ability can be improved upon over time through experience, training and the acquisition of new knowledge. Still, that requires effort over what might be an extended period, even for the most capable staffer. Resources, too, are not unlimited in any workplace or organization. In theory, if Resources were infinitely available and could be applied without additional marginal cost, Performance could be simply and significantly driven, but practically speaking this is not the case.

That leaves Motivation. An individual can realistically amplify their efforts through the simple experience of being highly engaged in a situation or workplace. As a manager or supervisor, despite what Herzberg might opine, you *can* directly influence and improve an individual's engagement through your interaction and leadership which in turn will multiply their Performance.

Lastly, it is worth noting that you can have a significant influence on employee motivation through the deft use of performance development tools including goal-setting and effective feedback, which we will discuss in detail in forthcoming chapters.

PART II

The Psychology of Performance Management

CHAPTER 8:

The Pygmalion Effect

"High achievement always takes place in the framework of high expectation."
—Charles Kettering, former head of research for General Motors

"Pygmalion in the Classroom," a then-controversial study conducted back in the 1960s by psychologists Robert Rosenthal and Lenore Jacobson, showed the strong co-relation that can take place between expectations and results[12].

The object of the study, in a nutshell, was for teachers to identify a randomly chosen group of students as "high achievers." These were not necessarily students who had a history of achievement – the idea was to *expect* them to achieve, and to make this expectation clear. Surely enough, at the end of the school year, the students in this group showed a remarkable improvement in their grade point average and IQ test scores.

The principles of the Pygmalion Effect are equally relevant in the modern workplace. Just as a student may conform to the expectation of a teacher, an employee may strive to achieve the expectations of a boss. If you offer a positive assessment, highlighting the areas you feel the employee is excelling in, and letting that person know they can achieve even more, it is likely that she will strive to live up to this image. Conversely, if an employee has been told he does inferior work, he might decide that this is the best he can do, and just give up trying altogether.

This isn't about lying to people. It's about focusing on development rather than shortcomings, and describing goals that you would like to see that employee achieve, using language that suggests you really believe it can happen. We build on strengths, not weaknesses.

Don't Say This	Say This!
"I know you've struggled learning the new system we've incorporated into the plant, but you just have to adapt the way everyone else has. Let's see if you can do better in the year to come."	"We've all had a big learning curve with this new system, but I've been very impressed with how hard you've tried to adapt to it. If you have any thoughts on how to make the process easier, I'd be pleased to hear them. I have a feeling that by the end of this year, you'll be an expert."
"You've had 6 months to take the Advanced SAP course, you need to make this a priority! If you can't upgrade your computer skills within the next month, I'll have to find someone who can."	"It's been such a hectic time for the business, and I know you haven't been able to fit in that SAP course. I appreciate how busy you are, but I rely so much on your expertise. Once you have that extra training I know you'll be a great help sharing your knowledge with our more junior staff."

"Why haven't these boxes been moved into the warehouse yet? They've been sitting here for three days! It's your job to keep this place organized, and instead it looks like disaster!"	"Thanks so much for all the work you do keeping this place organized – I know it's not an easy job with the volume of merchandise we have coming and going. I was hoping you might have some ideas on how we could have the warehouse better set up for shipping and receiving."
"This is the third day in a row you've had to leave early – I know you gave stuff going on but we're trying to run a business here and I feel like I just can't count on you anymore."	"I'm grateful that you've been able to come in to work despite the personal issues you've been having lately. I really respect what you're going through. But we have to keep the floor staffed at all times – do you have any ideas how we could make this work?"

In these examples we've taken employees who need a "gentle reminder" and phrased the expectation in such a way that they are the ones being asked for an idea or solution. We're setting a goal that is challenging, without being impossible, and expressing the belief that yes, they can do it! Be constructive and stay *positive* in tone. If you are fortunate enough to have employees who do not need any such reminder, there is still room for our friend Pygmalion. Just because someone is doing a great job without your intervention doesn't mean they don't need to hear a "kudos" every once in a while. Verbalize what they are doing well, and point out any areas that you feel they could successfully take a lead on.

In J. Sterling Livingston's article *Pygmalion in Management*[13] produced a year after Rosenthal and Jacobson's Thesis in 1969, he describes the powerful influence of a manager's expectation on employee behavior. Livingston, an outstanding Management Consulting expert and long-time professor at the Harvard Business School, spent a good part of his academic career studying the effects of managerial attitude on employee and organizational development. According to him, research reveals that *(this is a direct quote — I personally wouldn't use the word "subordinate," but it was the 1960's!)*:

❖ What managers expect of subordinates and the way they treat them largely determines their performance and career progress.

❖ A unique characteristic of superior managers is the ability to create high performance expectations that subordinates then fulfill.

❖ Less effective managers fail to develop similar expectations, and as a consequence, the productivity of their subordinates suffers.

❖ Subordinates, more often than not, appear to do what they believe they are expected to do.

While these theories may underestimate the self-determination of the "subordinate," they do provide useful insight into goal-setting and employee motivation. Pygmalion-style leadership is at work when employees excel in response to the belief that they are capable and indeed expected to do great things. As in many areas of life, what we project, and what we expect, can become a self-fulfilling prophesy.

The Pygmalion Effect isn't about having unrealistic expectations for a person. It also doesn't guarantee that you won't be let down by someone who is not willing or able to live up to the expectation you have projected. The key is to express goals that are attainable, and to establish a vision for a person that represents what their full potential *could* be.

Lastly, be mindful that the power of expectation works in both directions. If you have an employee experiencing performance challenges and you've exhausted all coaching opportunities, *and* have patiently engaged feedback strategies to bring about improvement without success, you may find yourself in a situation where you have to engage in a Performance Improvement Plan ("PIP") or similar process to formally document performance and bring about improvement. A balanced and healthy Performance Management System (and workplace culture, for that matter) requires this. Necessary though it may be, like the Pygmalion Effect, this type of feedback can also create a self-fulfilling prophecy. Approach PIPs with caution.

Why? In a PIP situation, discouraged by the lack of confidence their manager may be demonstrating towards their work, the employee experiences self doubt. In light of this new self consciousness, their performance may further diminish and their manager, now more focused on documentation of the newly minted PIP process, may abandon their primary and more important role as a leader and mentor in developing the employee's potential and empowering them to success. That is not only an employee failure, but a leadership failure.

This is not to say you should shy away from giving directional feedback to correct performance. When appropriate, you should. However, be mindful of potential impacts and tred lightly. The goal of constructive feedback is to correct undesirable behavior and to position the employee for future success. The last thing you want to do is undermine a team member's confidence and have them disengage.

CHAPTER 9:

Delivering Effective & Constructive Feedback

"The trouble with most of us is that we would rather be ruined by praise than saved by criticism."

— Norman Vincent Peale

Before we talk about feedback, I would like to define the concepts of Management and Leadership. Both agents require feedback tools to be successful in their missions. Management and leadership are not one in the same thing. Managers, "plan, direct, and control" things (and unfortunately, often people). Their influence is limited to their authority. While Managers may allow for some employee participation in decision making, they tend to make those calls alone, define work methods and centralize their authority. When Herzberg was talking about hygiene factors and the fact that supervisors and managers have little potential to engender positive motivation, he was referring to those that "manage", not those that provide leadership.

Leaders encourage autonomy. They involve employees in decision making, delegate their authority, and expect participation in deciding work methods. Leaders follow a new Golden rule which embraces the credo, "treat people the way *they* want to be treated" rather than "treat people the way *you* want to be treated".

Great Leaders do a lot of things right. They are very effective at providing their team with feedback. Feedback is an extremely powerful tool when delivered effectively. Providing feedback and recognition when things are going right is a more palatable exercise than taking corrective action when things are not moving in the right direction.

With that said, it's just as important to provide good feedback when staff have met or exceeded our expectations. Whether that feedback is provided at the moment of achievement or not is less important than ensuring the feedback is specific and direct so that it relates to the accomplishment and reinforces the behavior. Behavior that is recognized and reinforced is more likely to be repeated. Providing timely feedback in these circumstances increases commitment and engagement.

In the educational context, this is sometimes referred to as "descriptive feedback" which is simply feedback which provides students with a description of their learning. The transferability of this concept from classroom to workplace is seamless. The primary function of descriptive feedback is to improve employee self-awareness of their performance and to reduce any gaps between current performance levels and individual goals – ideally the same goals that the employee has established for themselves or finalized in consensus with their leader-manager. This type of supportive feedback will improve staff performance at an individual level, and at an organizational level it can contribute to a culture which embraces and optimizes performance as a built-in dynamic.

That's the relatively easy side of the feedback spectrum.

Let's talk about the other end of the spectrum. If you work with people, then you know that no one likes to be "criticized" and feedback offered in this spirit will fail in terms of having its intended effect. However, while providing constructive feedback is a difficult skill to master, if you are a manager you also know that you can't turn a blind eye when an employee is not living up to expectations, or worse still, doesn't have the information to realize and understand that this is the case. You will recall from Chapter 1 the important distinction between corrective action channels and developmental / growth channels. As mentioned there, it is important to establish upfront which side of the highway you wish to proceed down before leaving the driveway. Driving down the middle of the road often ends in calamitous results.

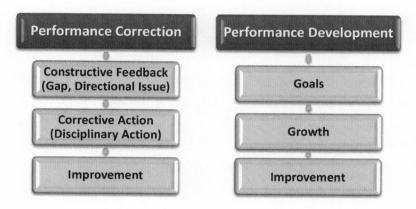

Performance situations that require you to take corrective action and to provide constructive feedback are challenging. No one takes pleasure in having to do so, but leaders recognize the necessity of this task to ensure their team knows where they stand and have an opportunity to improve. As a result, they have developed the ability to provide effective feedback over time. I've yet to meet a leader who possessed this skill innately or who developed it overnight. It is acquired with practice and experience.

If you feel uncomfortable or overwhelmed by the prospect of having to organize a discussion like this with one of your staff, rest assured that it does get easier the more often you engage in this type of dialogue. And if you don't immediately master its delivery, remember we all climbed the leadership ladder one mistake at a time.

Even if you have just recently recognized the need to provide constructive feedback, you know that these situations only tend to get worse, and you owe it to the rest of your staff to make sure everyone is pulling their weight equally. Likewise, everyone deserves to know if they are not meeting expectations and to be given the opportunity to improve, but this has to be communicated to them *first*. As with all difficult discussions, how you broach these conversations, and the intentions you communicate in so doing, is critical. Staying positive is key. Chances are, your employee will be doing a good job in some areas already, so this represents an opportunity to ensure they are performing consistently in all areas.

Here are some tips to help you give your employees the feedback they need (constructive or otherwise), without creating resentment.

1. Corrective feedback should be shared in a timely manner when the gap or directional issue is observed. Do not wait for the annual review process to bring issues forward. Not only is that unfair, it will undermine and diminish the developmental

potential of your performance discussion. Keep corrective action and development processes completely separate from one another. Always.

2. Make sure that you meet with the employee in a private setting. Your conversation should never be within earshot of other employees, or designed to openly embarrass the employee in question.

3. Set a relaxed tone for the conversation. If you approach an employee with an angry tone of voice, they will be more likely to go on the defensive and much less likely to listen openly to what it is you have to say.

4. Maintain eye contact. By physically stopping what you are doing and focusing completely on the person, they will be more likely to get the point that what you are saying is important. This also conveys sincerity and approachability.

5. Make sure you are engaged in a two-way discussion, not a one-way narrative. If you are still using a traditional evaluation system, they are almost exclusively focus on past performance and are characterized by one-way communication from the supervisor with too much time spent reviewing past shortcomings instead of planning for future successes. Some company forms that I have reviewed include an employee "rebuttal" section on the form. If your organization's process includes such a caveat, it is time to re-think your process from the bottom up.

6. Focus on the behavior or issue, not the person: No employee should ever leave a discussion feeling that you have personally attacked them. See Chapter 6 for more tips on how you can use wording that pinpoints specific actions, without targeting an employee's perceived shortcomings.

7. Get feedback from the employee. If you're dealing with a correctional issue, ask for ideas on how they feel the situation/behavior can be avoided in future. Let them know that you are always open to hearing what they have to say, and allow them to take personal responsibility for addressing and implementing solutions. It is their career, not yours. Let them assume ownership of their career.

8. Express your positive intent. If you have to give constructive feedback, the purpose is to correct a performance issue and to support improvement and development. If you need to take corrective action, it's just that, *corrective* action – not punishment or disciplinary action.

9. Get your facts straight and don't jump to unfounded conclusions. Make sure you are using Objective information and triangulating your facts. Previously in this book we also talked about Root Cause Analysis. Use it, and make sure it's an individual issue you're addressing and not a bi-product of a policy, practice or other environmental root cause.

10. Focus on results and keep the employee involved. Your team members are responsible for themselves – they are adults (usually) – let them take responsibility for performance issues

and independently develop tactics and solutions for resolving them. Your role as a leader is to provide the feedback they need to guide their development and to ensure they have the best environment and resources to be successful. You are a coach, a facilitator and at times an assessor, but you are not *responsible* for their careers or for solving all of their problems. Too often managers and supervisors believe it is their duty to solve everyone's problems – you are not a parent, spouse or a friend. Ensure you encourage and support autonomy and let your people take primary responsibility for their career path. While it may not be the most direct approach (especially if you're used to "managing"), your staff will respect you for it and you will build a more effective team and organization as a result.

11. Open and close with a compliment. By opening your exchange on a positive note, the employee will be more likely to accept your critique. By ending the exchange on a positive note, they will walk away without feeling that you are upset with them or that there may be further repercussions. At the same time, don't give a poor performer a 'good' review in hopes it will encourage improved performance.

The most important thing to remember any time you sit down with an employee for this type of exchange is to stick with the facts, and keep the dialogue as positive and constructive as you can. As we mentioned in Chapter 6, it's never about liking or disliking a person – we only deal in events and behaviors that are hampering performance, and your opinion about someone's personal qualities has nothing to do with it.

Unfortunately, there are times when delivering constructive feedback is more of a challenge than others. You know you have to be constructive and positive, but maybe an employee is really falling short on basic requirements and you have to honestly address the situation. Chances are, the employee knows they are falling short, but this doesn't mean it will be easy for them to hear about it.

In the following chart I have given a few examples of how you can handle these more difficult discussions. When there is problem behavior that needs to be addressed, the wording you choose can truly make or break the situation. As you can see, we have shifted the focus from personality to behavioral observation, and have provided concrete examples in each scenario of what the expectation is.

Don't Say This	Say This!
"You can be very rude, customers find you off-putting."	"A number of customers have indicated that you used inappropriate language during their visits. We want to ensure a great customer experience, so let's discuss what happened."
"People find you overly introverted. Why are you so quiet all the time?"	"It would be helpful if you participated more at the weekly staff meeting. I know you have great ideas and we want to hear them. I'd like you to share at least one of your ideas at our next staff meeting."

"You talk too much, it's disruptive to the other staff."	"I'm glad that you have friends here and are well-liked by the other staff, but we need to save non-work-related discussions for break time to make the best use of everyone's time and availability."
"That report was not helpful at all, I find your work is getting very sloppy."	"The content of your report was excellent but the layout and formatting could have been better organized. I know you were in a time-crunch on this one but in future I think it's worth it to spend more time on presentation."
"You're not being careful enough in the plant, someone is going to get injured and it will be your fault!"	"It can be hard to adhere to all the safety rules, but it's so important. Safety is our #1 priority in the plant or someone could be injured. We need to schedule some one-on-one time to go over our H&S policies and procedures. Let me know when you're free later today."
"Another client just called to say you made a mistake on their tax return! What's going on with you these days? I'm very disappointed with your lack of quality control!"	"This is our busiest time of year, but we have to take the time to review each client's file before signing off on it. You've always produced quality work in the past and we need to make sure you keep living up to that standard."

You are still getting your point across, but are delivering the message in a manner that will hopefully be better received by the employee. This doesn't mean they'll be happy to hear what you have to say, but they will at least not leave your discussion feeling that they have been personally insulted. You have also provided a tangible example of what your expectation is, and how they can achieve this.

Let's press these techniques into service with a working example. As with Goal Setting, below is a template you may wish to use when you are planning a discussion that will involve giving Constructive Feedback:

Constructive Feedback

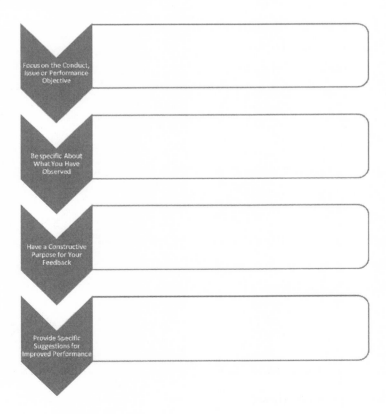

Let's practice these skills with another Case Study that calls for an application of these techniques.

CASE STUDY
Feedback Scenario One - Shirley

❖ Shirley has the most seniority in a social services organization and has been in the same position for nearly 20 years. Over the course of the last several months, she has been acting in an aggressive, uncooperative manner at work: Co-workers find her difficult and unapproachable.

❖ Her Manager has met with her several times – initially, "off-the-record" as a personal gesture to reach-out to Shirley, based on their long working relationship and given her loyalty within the agency. Nonetheless, efforts to extend assistance and to provide feedback have proven ineffective and the Manager, partially in frustration has told Shirley to "…just get your job done and get over your personal baggage."

❖ Following these dialogues and this particular comment, Shirley makes an allegation of harassment against her Manager, claiming among other things, that she's been singled-out for these discussions and that no other employees have been subjected to the same treatment. The harassment allegation is eventually resolved, however Shirley's performance continues to deteriorate.

❖ Provide Feedback to Shirley.

As before, I have included a Performance Plan to address these issue in the Appendices (however, try drafting your own solutions before checking out my take on this scenario). Remember, practice makes perfect (or as close as we can get to that ideal!)

Don't expect to be in a position to formulate complete and thoughtful feedback discussions right out of the gate. Start with the basics: developing strategies to rely on objective information as much as possible (triangulation), setting simple performance goals (model them out on paper using the 3-step process advised in this book), and giving descriptive feedback and recognition. You will find that if you layer, or scaffold your learning and the practice of these skills, your mastery of a basic activity will support and promote your achievement of the next level of performance development activity. Apply what you learn, and don't start with the most daunting and complex constructive feedback opportunity you have in front of you without first developing foundational competencies. Work from areas of comfort to develop more challenging areas of strength.

Feedback and the Appraisal Process

Though many of you may have an annual or other periodic performance appraisal process, once you have established and re-positioned your development process, I encourage you to think of these discussions as a *continuous* process, rather than an "event." Building an active performance development system into your culture will strengthen individual engagement and will deliver improved organizational effectiveness. Consider having formal (and informal) discussions about performance throughout the year. It has been said that twelve 10-minute discussions can have a greater impact than one 120-minute discussion.

84

Based on nearly twenty years of HR practice and working with people, it is my observation that one of the most important skill any leader can possess -- and the one many of us struggle to develop -- is providing candid and effective feedback. It's not easy and it's not a task most of us look forward to. For those of you in this camp, I provide a final Case Study on the next page to help you practice this critical skill (a solution is provided in the Appendices).

❖ Karen is a Project Manager in a growing Consulting Engineering firm that provides services to industrial and municipal clients. She is a classic "over-achiever" who frequently receives performance bonuses based on the impact of her work.

❖ She spends long hours at the office and produces an exceptional amount of work at a consistently high level of quality. With that said, there are some areas of concern. She is a high detail-person and sometimes focuses too much on fine points which can unnecessarily delay the completion of a project or task for others who depend on her to complete project tasks before they can move forward with their own work.

❖ Karen can be "short" with co-workers who don't work at her level (she prefers working alone). She dismisses company procedures that she doesn't agree with as "bureaucracy" and can be abrasive when working on team projects, disregarding the input and opinions of colleagues on the team.

❖ Provide Feedback to Karen.

As mentioned at the beginning of this Chapter, while corrective feedback is sometimes needed to realign employee performance, make sure that this isn't your exclusive performance management tool. Positive feedback and reinforcement are critical to developing a high performance work environment where staff feel respected, acknowledged and committed to the organization. If your performance evaluation process is focused on identifying gaps and things done wrong, you may wish to reconsider what your role as a leader is within the organization. Shouldn't your most important role as a leader be improving the effectiveness of your team and developing their capabilities? If you cannot honestly identify what is the focus of your performance evaluation system (and your leadership model), then you've got it wrong. As a leader, you are accountable (or should be) for your staff's performance and their effectiveness within the organization. Your interests should be so aligned in your performance review system.

CHAPTER 10:

Conducting an Effective Performance Development Discussion

"The only real mistake is the one from which we learn nothing."
– Henry Ford

We've already outlined some specifics on how to deliver effective feedback in Chapter 9. Orchestrating an effective Performance Discussion requires a mastery of these techniques to ensure the best results. A Performance Discussion is not a quick exchange made with certain employees as problems arise, but is a vehicle for ensuring that everyone on your team (especially those individuals who are not always knocking on your door), get a chance to dialogue with you in a meaningful way.

Performance Discussions should be conducted with all employees, but as advised in our first chapter, decide what it is you are trying to achieve with this discussion (are you looking to *correct* a problem, or are you interested in having a *development* discussion). Here are some basic steps you may want to follow to create the right environment for an effective Performance Discussion:

1. Create a relaxed environment. Don't rush the conversation.

2. Always allow the employee to complete a 'pre-appraisal' before commencing any formal development process. This is a key step, and one that should not be overlooked. Top-down processes that exclude employee input on the front-end have been consistently debunked, and are ineffective. Moreover, unless you are conducting a development discussion with only one employee, you will find that having the onus of drafting several one-way performance reviews is a time-consuming and daunting activity. Inviting employee input not only makes your discussion a more effective *dialogue*, on a practical level you will also find that this greatly reduces the amount of energy and time you will invest in this process, and it will allow you to instead focus that energy on coaching and facilitating performance improvement.

3. Allow employees an opportunity to bring up any issues or concerns that they might have. Show that you are being attentive by listening carefully and taking notes during pre-appraisal discussions. If you weren't born a great listener, you may want to consider practicing 'Active Listening' – an effective listening technique long used by therapists and counselors, and in conflict resolution situations. This technique requires the listener to repeat or paraphrase what they heard from the speaker to confirm understanding and to ensure an accurate reception of ideas. It can go a long way to minimizing or eliminating misunderstandings and is a great way to reflect on and process information during a discussion with staff.

4. Ask employees for ideas they have to address issues they have brought to your attention. You do not need to have a solution for everyone's problems. Your role as a leader is to create opportunities for professional growth and to provide appropriate resources for making that happen. Employees are adults, and they are individuals. They are principally responsible for their own career development, not you! Your performance development systems should recognize and encourage that type of (supported) independence. If you have not already done so, transfer ownership of the process back to the employees, where it belongs.

5. Have any documentation relating to Performance Appraisals, Objectives or Assessments for that employee on hand. Focus on objective results and observations as much as possible –avoid gearing the conversation to their personality. If there are areas requiring improvement, or identified as development opportunities, ask for the employee's thoughts on how this can be achieved. Encourage the employee to take ownership for identifying the means to achieve these outcomes. If you find yourself giving corrective or directional feedback, make sure your dialogue is occurring outside of your development process, and not as part of that system.

6. Focus as much as possible on strengths which can be further developed. Use non-judgmental language that emphasizes results, rather than dwelling on behavior that has occurred in the past. While we should not completely disregard the past, remember that *development* is a forward-facing activity. Too often, feedback

systems dwell on past performance issues and fixing what went wrong. While I am not suggesting that you should overlook critical shortcomings, make sure you are using the right set of tools to do the job. Performance correction discussions have their time and place – a development discussion isn't the time to drag out those tools. Remember, driving performance to new levels requires you to look through the windshield at what's coming instead of fixating on traffic in the rearview mirror.

7. Goals and expectations that are established should be clear, concise, and achievable. Make sure you DOT goals that are agreed upon with your employee.

8. Development discussions also represent a good opportunity to review any professional development or training plans with the employee that may support goal achievement and personal growth. Training and experience opportunities may be critical to an individual's achievement of goals or their development plan, so it makes sense to integrate and identify training needs in your development system.

9. Finally, summarize the key points of your conversation and end the meeting on a positive note, perhaps mentioning one last time any areas that they have really excelled in since your last discussion.

In short, performance discussions are not about you recounting everything the employee has done right and wrong – it is about giving employees an opportunity to voice their own ideas on how they can further develop themselves professionally, and possible steps that might be taken to allow this to happen. In other words, don't just talk, listen! Properly handled, Performance Management is one of the most powerful opportunities to engage your staff in a way that also strengthens your own relationship with them, and their affinity with the organization.

Rating Scales

I don't like rating scales, but most of my clients do. We have all been socialized from grade school to place tremendous importance on marks and performing to pre-determined standards. Typically these standards are assessed by a single individual (a teacher, or our manager). As such it seems logical that our development systems should likewise have grades or rating scales. Traditionally, most performance appraisal systems had (and still have) some kind of static rating scale: "1 – 10", "Meets", "Does Not Meet", "Exceeds" – and the like. This also explains why many of the performance evaluation and appraisal systems that we audit seem relatively juvenile in their outlook, perhaps harkening back to our parochial elementary school roots.

Moreover, when we receive feedback from staff and their managers concerning their existing systems, they focus almost exclusively on the lack of objectivity in the rating scales and the inconsistency in their application across the organization (*"Bill got a 4.5 and I only received a 4, yet I produce more than Bill and he is late everyday…"*). Rarely do we hear concerns expressed about the value of having development discussions and receiving feedback. To the contrary, the vast majority of employees (especially high performers) long for honest feedback and the opportunity to express plans for the future. This type of dialogue with their manager is a must-have. Too often we see completed performance evaluations that simply have "the boxes checked" for each factor's rating scale with very little thought or effort being made in the "comments" section.

In our view, the so-called comments section is the most important part of any performance discussion. It is, or should be, the heart of any development dialogue. It is in this too-often overlooked area of the review form that the opportunity to have a fluid and constructive dialogue of performance is missed. For this reason, and given the illogical presence of the "rating scale" (beyond nostalgia for the school yard), that we recommend removing rating scales entirely.

Clients who have accepted this recommendation have found it liberating. Not only does it remove a beef many staff have with their old evaluation system, it also takes the pressure off managers to "defend" the ratings employees received (especially when employees compare their ratings with peers – and they do – to seek justification for differences in their 'marks'). Most importantly though, it re-focuses the discussion on where it should be: on development and on the employee's realized and planned achievements towards factors that have been identified as most important for organizational success. Creating an opportunity for staff to have a candid and meaningful two-way conversation with their manager is (or should be) the most critical mission in every development system.

The Factors

Clients often ask me if there is a standardized set of factors that should be employed to organize performance discussions. As mentioned above, I don't agree with rating people on a "scale of 1-10", but I do offer below a set of commonly used performance factors that can be applied to many positions and organizations. These performance factors cover everything from communication style to technical ability. You can choose your own.

As with other aspects of your performance system, I highly recommend that you involve staff in the design and content of your own system. If they have ownership, you will get buy-in. The integrity of your system is critical for it to be viewed and used as an effective method, and this lack of credibility in many organizations explains the bad rap many performance evaluations systems have earned.

One very simple way to involve your employees in the set-up of your system is to create a simple, and preferably anonymous, survey to ask them which factors they view as most relevant to their individual success and that of your organization. When we are repositioning a client's development system, we always survey employees to collect this input.

I have included numerous categories here (in no particular order) – naturally you can choose the ones which best apply to your organization. The list is by no means exhaustive and is representative of a more comprehensive library of factors we maintain when tailoring systems in different organizations. This should get you started if you're looking at creating or re-positioning your current system.

KEY PERFORMANCE FACTORS (examples)

1. QUALITY OF WORK

Work is organized, neat and well thought-out. Employee takes pride in the work produced and extensive revision is rarely required. Work is checked carefully and is predominantly error-free. The overall quality of work is comparable to that of the rest of the team.

2. JOB KNOWLEDGE

Demonstrates expert-level understanding of all required skills. Employee is well informed about the department in which he/she works, and understands the organizational expectations and practices that are required to excel at their job.

3. SUPERVISION REQUIRED

Consistently achieves results and produces high-quality work with minimum supervision required. He/she is capable of working independently with minimal outside support. Employee does not require constant direction to remain fully engaged in work activities.

4. EFFICIENCY

Plans and organizes work assignments efficiently. Completes work on-time or before deadlines. He/she respects timelines and consistently produces the required volume of work in accordance with pre-determined work schedules. Employee respects the importance of adhering to timelines to achieve organizational goals.

5. MOTIVATION

Defines appropriate goals, works toward achieving these goals, and is able to articulate vision and steps required for achievement. He/she is capable of looking at the "bigger picture" and envisioning a desired end-result.

6. ATTENDANCE

Rarely misses work without a viable reason, and is consistently on time when the workday begins. Employee is available when needed and ensures regular attendance at all work functions, including special events and meetings. He/she sometimes arrives at work early or stays late during periods when there is a critical deadline to be met.

7. RELIABILITY

Has the willingness and ability to meet work expectations in a timely manner, and gives sufficient notice when this is not possible. He/she can be depended upon to follow through on their word and carry out the responsibilities which they have committed to.

8. PLANNING & ORGANIZATION

Understands and follows charts, schedules and instructions. Employee keeps thoroughly accurate and complete records. He/she has the ability to accurately prioritize planned or routine work, and can also manage unplanned work when required.

9. INNOVATION & ADAPTABILITY

Ability to continuously improve and troubleshoot within his/her own work area, accept change and manage the unexpected. Finds ways to perform work more efficiently. Employee generates creative ideas and is resourceful when managing new projects or issues.

10. JUDGEMENT & ACCOUNTABILITY

Makes logical and reasonable job-related decisions. Employee admits to mistakes and learns from them. He/she consistently demonstrates sound judgement and an ability to take action in an appropriate manner as issues arise.

11. VALUES & PRINCIPLES

Demonstrates support and commitment to their employer, co-workers, managers and customers. Employee is consistently dependable, maintains confidentiality, and can be counted on by the team. He/she demonstrates positive core-values and ethics such as honesty, integrity, and loyalty.

12. CUSTOMER FOCUS & SATISFACTION

Demonstrates a commitment to exceeding customer expectations and supporting the organization's goal of ensuring complete customer satisfaction. He/she possesses the communication and interpersonal skills to work effectively with customers, and to deal with complaints or problem situations as they occur.

13. BUSINESS DEVELOPMENT

Respects and achieves sales plan goals, strives to maintain quota, and possesses a solid understanding of the marketplace. He/she works to meet prospect/customer needs, and has effective promotional, opening and closing techniques.

14. REVENUE GENERATION

Has a proven track record of success in meeting and exceeding financial goals. He/she plays an important role in the financial achievement of the organization.

15. BUDGETARY ACCOUNTABILITY

Uses resources efficiently, strives to reduce cost, and maintains an active interest in and knowledge of the internal budgeting process. He/she has a basic understanding of planned sales volumes and revenues, resource quantities, costs and expenses, assets, liabilities and cash flows, as relevant to his/her position or department.

16. PRODUCT OR SUBJECT-MATTER EXPERTISE

Demonstrates a strong understanding of the product or service being provided by his/her employer. The employee is capable of clearly communicating the features, benefits, technical details, and comparative marketplace information relevant to this product or service.

17. POSITIVE ATTITUDE

Displays a positive and pleasant disposition and outlook. Employee does not allow personal problems or conflicts to hinder work activities, and attempts to maintain an agreeable attitude when interacting with others.

18. INITIATIVE

Takes action, seeks new opportunities, and strives to see projects to completion. He/she has the ability to work independently, produce results and make decisions with minimal outside influence.

19. PERSONAL LEARNING

Quickly and succinctly applies new knowledge and skills to the job. Employee actively and positively participates in technical or administrative changes. He/she asks for opportunities to learn or train, and takes initiative in finding opportunities for professional development.

20. COMMUNICATION SKILLS

Effectively listens to others, and has a strong ability to convey and receive ideas, information and direction. He/she solicits feedback from others when making important decisions. Employee effectively expresses information in one-on-one and group situations, and has the ability to communicate clearly both orally and in writing.

21. INTERPERSONAL SKILLS

Builds strong relationships and listens to what others have to say. He/she functions effectively in a team setting and is able to work cooperatively and collaboratively with individuals at all levels of the organization. Generally, this person is well liked by co-workers, management and clients/customers.

22. CONFLICT MANAGEMENT

Possesses strong listening skills, and an ability to understand where other people are coming from. He/she is committed to finding solutions to problems, and works well with difficult people and strong personality-types.

23. TEAMWORK

The employee is able to work collaboratively with co-workers, managers, clients and/or customers. He/she supports the team in all work-related activities and demonstrates an interest in helping others to achieve their goals.

24. PROBLEM-SOLVING

Possesses the ability to clearly isolate, define and troubleshoot problem areas. Employee overcomes obstacles and effectively identifies problems in order to meet objectives or find alternative solutions. Decisions are made with a timely and logical approach that is based on information given.

25. HEALTH & SAFETY COMPLIANCE

Possesses a strong familiarity with Health & Safety policies. Employee exercises personal responsibility in complying with organizational policies and procedures as they relate to health and safety. Works with a safety conscious attitude and demonstrates good practices. He/she takes responsibility for reporting incidents and accidents in a timely manner.

26. COMPUTER SKILLS

Possesses a solid understanding of the software packages required for his/her job, and takes advantage of new technology as it becomes available. He/she learns new tools quickly, and uses technology to enhance job performance.

27. TECHNICAL SKILLS

Maintains current understanding of technical processes, tools and equipment, and uses technology to increase performance and productivity. He/she demonstrates a commitment to keeping these skills up-to-date as technology evolves.

28. PROJECT MANAGEMENT

Monitors status of projects, thoroughly deals with project issues as they arise, holds team members accountable for performance, and delivers a clear, accurate interpretation of project status and deliverables.

29. SELF DEVELOPMENT

Looks for opportunities to increase knowledge, take on additional responsibility, and achieve personal goals. He/she takes advantage of personal development opportunities as they present themselves, and strives to continuously improve themselves professionally.

30. STRATEGIC THOUGHT

Works to establish and articulate a strategic vision, and shows creativity when outlining solutions. He/she has the ability to think long-term while keeping an end-goal in mind.

31. DECISION MAKING

Demonstrates the ability to reach decisions, and consider numerous factors involved before coming to a conclusion. He/she takes a thoughtful approach when evaluating options, seeks input from others, and can make a decision even when there are difficult circumstances involved.

This significant inventory should get you started! There are many more and no one set of factors is more "right" than another, it all depends on the unique culture and scope of your organization. When allowing employees to pick the key performance factors that they feel apply to them, clients are often concerned that employees will not select factors relevant or important to their business. Don't be. In my experience, employees understand their organization and almost always pick the same factors as the managers and business owners do. However, if you are a manufacturer, and no one selects "Health and Safety," you probably have other problems!

Ultimately, it is less important which factors are selected and more important that there is a meaningful and candid dialogue between managers and staff members. The focal point of that discussion (the Factor) is secondary to the larger exchange of ideas, development of rapport and understanding that occurs in this forum. The environmental conditions of the development conversation are also important: namely, everything discussed in this book so far as it respects employee motivation, cues, having effective conversations, goal setting, feedback and so on. Really it is less important that you're having a conversation about "Quality of Work" or "Innovation" and more important that this dialogue is facilitated in a way that stays true to the concepts and tools we have already reviewed.

The final area I am often asked about concerning Key Performance Factors is the number of factors that should be included in your system. Again, there is no right or wrong answer here. It is organization specific. In my experience, fewer than five factors tends to not create a wide enough scope for dialogue, while more than ten can lead to a lack of focus. Having said this, we have clients with outstanding performance systems that don't fit within these range limits. Do what's right for your staff and your organization.

CHAPTER 11:

Fostering Self-Direction

"When you talk, you are only repeating what you already know; but when you listen, you learn something new."

– Dalai Lama

As we reviewed earlier, the central tenet of *management*, historically, has been "plan-control-direct." Yes, employees will often do what you tell them to do, but perhaps that's all they're doing – the bare minimum. Are they excelling at problem solving and quality control? Are they volunteering for team building sessions and special task forces? Are they innovating and coming up with ideas on how to save your organization time or money? Maybe. Maybe not.

The "plan-control-direct" mindset worked wonders in the development of the systematic management systems which drove Western industrialization and manufacturing to never-before-seen productivity. However, even the later refinements to these strategies by the first management consultants of the early 20th Century, such as industrial engineer Frederick Taylor, did not address the fundamental need that employees have to be self actualizing and fulfilled in their work.

Some would argue that the very presence of a manager actually nips this self-actualization process in the bud. How can you be self-actualizing with someone constantly looking over your shoulder, telling you what to do? In fact planning, controlling and directing every move you make?

Many Fortune 500 companies have effectively implemented "self-directed teams," a concept which involves teams working independently to problem-solve and take corrective action with minimal or sometimes no input at all from a traditional manager. These work teams are given direct access to the information and resources they need to control and improve their operation, project or work area. Instead of parceling out work responsibilities in smaller increments, tasks become restructured around larger organizational functions, with an end-goal in mind. Studies have shown that organizations which employ this type of autonomous work system can show a remarkable increase in productivity, with employees reporting less boredom and workplace dissatisfaction (Business Week, April 2016).

So does this mean we don't need managers after all? While there is no doubt value in the concept of a Self Directed Team, such a dramatic shift in organizational structure seems a bit over the top for the average business. However, few could refute the value of creating a workforce that does not require micro-management. A manager should be dealing with the bigger-picture issues of running a profitable business, or an effective not-for-profit agency, not worrying about every move being made by her team of direct reports.

While establishing Self Directed Teams might not be the right answer for your workplace, the principles of this work structure has a lot to offer: Giving your employees more autonomy and decision making ability allows you to save time on the resolution of small-scale problems, and more time for the strategic thinking and large-scale goal setting that will propel your organization forward.

Self Directed Teams may require a significant upfront investment in additional training and a higher caliber of talent. To be autonomous, the individuals on the team will require problem solving, decision making and self-regulation skills. If full self-direction is not realistic for the size or scope of your workplace, think about smaller ways in which you can foster greater autonomy for your employees:

❖ Set up assignments and projects around results or outcomes. State what the end goal is, but do not become involved until the final stages, if at all. Once you have explained the point of achieving the project goal in a bigger corporate or organizational context, step back and see what they can do. Often, the team momentum behind a project pushes employees to work even harder than they would if a supervisor was overseeing them.

❖ Recognize that not everyone is a team player. You no doubt have a few employees who prefer to work on their own. This does not have to be a negative – find a niche for them, perhaps a project that requires individual effort, research or extensive documentation. Work to strengths. These are often the employees who put their head down and end up going above and beyond what is required without the distraction of other people around. Team diversity makes for stronger and more resilient teams.

❖ Be quick to acknowledge initiative and self-discipline when you see it. If an employee or team has taken charge of a project or troubleshooting issue, provide as much praise and support as possible to keep the ball rolling. Openly recognize all achievements. Make sure they know how much you appreciate their contribution, and perhaps provide a reward if appropriate. Remember, a reward does not always need to be monetary: it could be a special lunch, time off, tickets to a conference or workshop, a committee leadership role, a personal development opportunity, or even a simple "thank you". Don't underestimate the impact of "thank you" or miss an opportunity to offer one.

❖ Don't lose sight of the fact that the people who work for you are adults! Many of your employees manage to raise children, run a home and pay bills, so is it really such a stretch that they should be able to take charge in the workplace as well? Give them the opportunity whenever possible to provide input about any decision affecting their work area. Hold focus groups periodically (i.e. to review policy manuals, potential software upgrades, or any other changes that might affect staff) so that employees have a formal venue where their thoughts and ideas can be shared.

❖ Don't skimp on training and development. Training in problem solving, leadership and process improvement, as examples, can be a great way to spark the desire in your employees to go above and beyond what is expected of them in their day-to-day work tasks. Development programs do not need to be expensive to have an impact.

❖ Create a "safe zone" for ideas. Your employees will not feel comfortable suggesting changes and taking the lead on initiating them if they feel that there will be a negative consequence should the idea fail. Sometimes even the most well-thought-out plans don't work in practice. Moreover, while not every idea should necessarily be carried out, every idea should at least be listened to with respect. A good idea that is not feasible at the moment can always be put on hold for when the budget allows. Avoid imposing corrective action when someone makes a mistake. Employees in organizations that follow this practice never take risks. The opportunity for innovation and progress will be compromised if your staff don't at least occasionally take risks to improve the mousetrap.

❖ Don't overlook lower-level staff. The more mundane or task-oriented a job is, the more satisfaction the employee derives from feeling that they have some autonomy in their role. Being given the opportunity to develop their own work plan methods or timelines can go a long way towards improving morale.

❖ Make sure your employees have the tools they need to work comfortably and independently. If you think you are saving money by not investing in technology upgrades, health and wellness programming, or other tools that facilitate the day-to-day operation of your business, think again. The cost in employee turnover and lost productivity may outweigh the cost of these relatively small, up-front expenditures. Ask your employees what they think they need to be able to do their jobs better. It doesn't necessarily mean adding a massage therapist to your head count, but your staff's feedback will provide you with cues about what is important to them.

If self-directed work is not an option for you across the board, at least consider some of these concepts to reshape the way you organize work.

Employing a combination if these tactics will hopefully help to foster an environment where your more junior and mid-level employees have greater ownership of the tasks they perform or services they deliver. It will also create a greater pool of crossed-trained employees to cover absences or sudden gaps in staffing. At a minimum, you will be able to take your vacation time without worrying about your business or department falling apart!

PART III

Difficult Decisions

Chapter 12:

Making the Tough Call

"Courage is being scared to death, but saddling up anyways."

– John Wayne

So you've used Root Cause Analysis, given constructive feedback, triangulated all of your data, engaged in performance development, set goals and performance objectives, created self-directed work teams, and you've even read up on Pygmalion! The results in your workplace have been very positive, and you've noticed that your staff seem motivated and engaged in their work.

Except for Joe. You've talked to Joe so many times, using all of your fine-tuned performance management strategies, but Joe just doesn't seem to be buying in to any of it. Perhaps Joe has problems outside of work that you don't know anything about, or maybe the type of work he is doing is just not the right fit for his personality or skill set. The point is, you have given him every opportunity to prove himself and he hasn't come through.

No manager wants to have "that conversation" – it is extremely uncomfortable, an admission to yourself and to your other staff that you made a mistake hiring that person, and also marks the beginning of a long recruiting process. But before you go any further down the corrective action road of your performance management system, make sure you're not at fault. As a team leader, your #1 responsibility is supporting and facilitating the success of your team, and by definition the individuals on your team. Have you met that fiduciary duty to your staff? Be honest with yourself. We've established that your staff have a self-directed responsibility for their own development and career path, but you are the guardian for ensuring they have the (available) resources to enable success. You must work with them to ensure those goals align with overall organizational priorities. If they've strayed from these targets and expectations for behavior, have you fulfilled your coaching and feedback responsibilities to ensure correction? A team member's failure is your failure as a leader if you haven't met these essential mandates.

Assuming you have met your primary leadership responsibilities, if you have arrived at the point where you feel you need to fire someone, you must have good reason. Obvious deal-breakers include verbal or physical abuse of other employees, theft, or some other form of serious deception – but then you don't need to be an HR expert to figure that out! If you have gone through all of the communication, feedback and improvement plan processes to correct the behavior, you may be left with no other choice than termination. Some typical "problem employee" profiles we see in the workplace may include:

❖ A perniciously negative attitude. Negativity can spread to your other employees like a disease, and the drama that often goes along with it can de-motivate even the best people on your team. Do you have an employee who never stops complaining, who stirs the pot of dissatisfaction with co-workers, who is argumentative, and who refuses to participate in organizational initiatives? These types of behavior must be confronted early on to ensure they don't escalate. Without intervention, this person is going to drag down everyone on your team. Intervene early with feedback.

❖ **Absenteeism, especially in their first year of employment.** It's never okay to miss a lot of work without a very good reason, but if an employee has recently started a job and is already calling in with excuses, this is a bad omen of what is to come. If a person routinely misses time every month (without medical justification) and the behavior has not improved in subsequent months despite verbal and written warnings, this is a red flag that should not be ignored.

❖ **Poor behavior that is getting worse.** None of us are without fault, and we all make mistakes at work at some point in our career, but if you have had several discussions with an employee about a particular action or behavior, and you are not seeing any signs of improvement, you should be concerned. If feedback, written warnings and structured Performance Improvement Plans (PIPs) do not bring about a correction you will have to consider other options.

❖ **You are receiving complaints about an employee from other members of your staff.** Don't exclusively rely on hearsay, but listen to what your other employees have to say. If someone seems nice enough to you but NO ONE else is getting along with him, you may need to take a closer look at this individual's workplace conduct. "Personality Conflict" is a good example of behavior that can often be corrected with coaching, but if the person has not responded to your intervention, you have to think about how the situation might be affecting the work performance of your other staff.

- ❖ **You are receiving complaints about an employee from clients or customers.** The only thing worse than hearing criticism of an employee from your staff is hearing it from the people you rely on to pay the bills! While chances do need to be given, it sends out the wrong message to your customers if you keep a person on board who has had negative interactions with them in the past, and who shows no desire to improve. It tells customers that they are not important, and you run the risk of losing them. If several clients/customers have complained, then action must be taken.

- ❖ **Unreasonable demands.** It is often the case that when an employee starts to become disenchanted with his job, and is perhaps thinking about leaving anyway, he will begin to approach you with demands that are not realistic for your workplace. Learn to recognize this for what it is: the employee is trying to see what he can get away with, and is willing to run the risk of being fired.

As a manager or business leader, going through the termination process is one of the most difficult and sometimes heart-wrenching endeavors you will have to undertake. This is particularly true if you are running a smaller business, where close relationships with staff can be quickly forged. Being the boss, however, means following through on tough decisions for the welfare of your organization and for the benefit of the rest of your team. Think about it this way: you would not be doing yourself or the ill-suited employee in question any favors by keeping them in a job that they are clearly not suited for. Not only could this be disastrous for your business, but it could keep that person from pursuing an opportunity or life goal that is more truly in alignment with what they were meant to do. These decisions should be made during the probationary period, or at least within the employee's first year of working for you. There are few things more difficult to deal with, not to mention unfair to all parties involved, than finally broaching an issue 5-10 years into the relationship.

So, you've recognized the warning signs and realize that it would be in the best interest of all parties to dismiss a member of your staff. What is the best way to go about doing this? Are there possible legal implications? How much severance do you need to pay, if any? What kind of paperwork needs to be filed? It's definitely not enough to just say "You're fired!"

Hopefully you have addressed these issues already (i.e. an employment contract and probationary period), but even if you do, the dismissal of an employee is a scenario that must be handled with considerable care. Even if you think that person is utterly incompetent, if you are firing them for the wrong reasons, or in the wrong way, you may be required to pay significant legal damages, not to mention causing unnecessary distress to all parties involved. Short of going out of business, being sued is every employer's worst nightmare, so it is certainly worth taking some precautionary measures to help ensure the situation doesn't come to this. Moreover, regardless of the circumstances or the culpability of the employee, the impact of this decision will place them in a very vulnerable situation and you need to recognize and provide appropriate support to them during this transition.

Below are some guidelines you may consider:

❖ If you are within the probationary period (which should be detailed in the employee's Employment Contract), then this process just got a lot easier. You have a right to let an employee go within this time period if you feel, for any reason at all, that they are not a good fit. Some probationary periods are as short as one month – I personally recommend a three-month probationary period, in writing, because it can often take this long for a busy manager to figure out that an employee is just not fitting in, or that they are not developing into a role at a reasonable pace. Always seek the advice of a lawyer or other expert to ensure your probationary periods comply with any pertinent employment laws or regulations.

❖ I can't over-emphasize the importance of having a well-written employment agreement for every member of your team. If you don't have a qualified Human Resources person on staff, it is well worth the expense of having this written up by a qualified consultant or an employment lawyer. In addition to outlining a probationary period, there must be a detailed description of the employee's obligations to your organization. If this is in writing, then the relationship is clearly understood, as will be the respective obligations of the employer and employee should that relationship come to an end.

❖ If it is too late for this (i.e. you never had a contract in place but really need to let someone go), the person can be terminated for just cause, with reasonable notice, or payment in lieu of notice (more on this below). There is no guarantee, however, that the employee will not take the legal route, but if you have carefully documented their shortcomings or misconduct at work and have given them a fair opportunity to improve, you will at least be in a better position to justify your decision.

❖ Just Cause: Some reasons for firing an employee are more clear-cut than others. If someone has been caught stealing, for example, you may be able to let them go without notice. You must pay them any amounts owing, but you have no further responsibility to them. The difficulty is, however, establishing "Just Cause" in the court system. It rarely happens. The law always favors the employee (mostly for good reason), so you must have considerable proof to solidify your case. Moreover, if you allege cause in termination and fail to sufficiently backstop your allegation, you are potentially exposing yourself to additional legal consequences. For this reason, many employers shy away from alleging cause unless there are clear, black-and-white facts to substantiate such a case.

These are exceptional cases, and if you have a strong performance management system in place, it should rarely be the case that you need to deal with a complex legal issue. However, if you do, **the longer and stronger your paper trail is the better.** There must be written documentation of warnings that have been issued, opportunities that have been provided for that person to improve, chances they have been given to explain themselves, complaints made by customers (for example), and any other concrete proof you can provide to show that all avenues have been explored. Moreover, the employee must absolutely be made aware of any information (in writing) with the opportunity to explain their conduct - and, importantly, with an opportunity to correct and improve upon their performance (after all, as an employer, that is what you want to see happen!). Because of the significant procedural and evidential burdens involved, we rarely see clients allege "cause", hence the frequent use of severance packages and releases.

- ◆ Payment in Lieu of Notice: If there is a clause for this in the employee's contract, the amount he will get paid is already decided. If not, you and the employee will need to agree on an amount that is satisfactory enough for him to leave without a fuss. Sometimes it is in the employee's best interest to leave early and she will agree to a reasonable amount. This is not usually the case, so you might have a problem on your hands. Take some comfort in the knowledge that most people want to leave a job on good terms, in the hopes of at least getting a reference. As long as you are being fair, and considering factors such as length of service, you are likely to come to an agreement in short order. In many cases, the employer is not strictly required to offer a termination package to the employee, but does so anyway. Sometimes it is worth this relatively small expense to make a clean break.

Please note that the above is an oversimplified summary of the sometimes enormously complex issues that can emerge if you have to end an employment relationship in difficult circumstances.

120

A Performance Management System can protect you from these risks to a large extent, but they cannot always completely eliminate the risk. For this reason, it is advisable that you consult with a qualified employment lawyer if you should find yourself in a situation that requires you to pursue these actions.

I've deliberately addressed this topic in a relatively superficial w ay, because "how to fire people" is not the focus of this book. Hopefully, the information discussed will help you avoid these situations, with termination (after the probationary period) rarely being required. An effective Performance Management System, which we have attempted to describe in this work, will minimize the potential for there to be misunderstandings and performance gaps in your workplace. Where these arise, hopefully the techniques we have outlined will support you in managing these disconnects and will realign expectations and performance in the agreed direction.

No one comes to work wanting to do a bad job. The overwhelming majority of employees want to achieve success and be recognized for their contributions. Performance Management will provide the ecosystem to support this goal. Make sure your communication and feedback systems are active and responsive to set the table for organizational success.

CHAPTER 13:

Turning the Tables

"You can't build a reputation on what you are going to do."
– Henry Ford

The lines of constructive communication must go both ways: As a manager, you have every opportunity to discuss the performance of your staff, but are they being given the same opportunity? Maybe you're a little reticent to know what your employees really think about you. It's probably not as bad as you think, but how do you know? Just the fact that you are reading a book on this topic indicates that you have an above-average concern for your employees, which they have surely already picked up on. However, if someone does have a problem with you, or with another manager in your organization, it's better to find out early and deal with it.

We are frequently asked to conduct employee engagement surveys, and truly feel like this is a great chance for employees to have a voice when it comes to how their workplace is run, and how they really perceive their managers. I recommend that these surveys always be anonymous, and conducted by a third party – it is the only way you will get honest and unbiased feedback. Typically I present these as a combination of multiple choice questions, and include an opportunity to post additional comments.

Below is an example of a basic "employee to supervisor" survey which is standard enough to use in just about any workplace. These would take a multiple choice form (i.e.: Very, Not Very, or Always, Sometimes, Never, depending on the question).

1. How approachable is your supervisor?

2. How available to employees is your supervisor?

3. How often does your supervisor give you feedback about your work?

4. Has your performance improved after receiving feedback from your supervisor?

5. How effective is the training you receive?

6. How consistently does your supervisor recognize employees for good work?

7. Does your supervisor take too much time to make decisions, too little time, or about the right amount of time?

8. How often does your supervisor listen to employees' opinions when making decisions?

9. How easy is it for employees to disagree with the decisions made by your supervisor?

10. How realistic are the expectations of your supervisor?

11. How well does your supervisor respond to employees' mistakes?

12. How reliable is your supervisor?

13. How effectively does your supervisor use organizational resources?

This is a very basic survey – you may want to go into more detail, or add content that is specific to the nature of your business. The idea is to keep the line of questioning objective, and have standardized responses that can be translated into empirical data. This allows for trends to be drawn between different management styles, and for certain "problem issues" to be brought into focus.

If you decide to do an independent staff survey without the help of an outside party, the most essential aspect to remember is complete confidentiality. Not too many employees will be 100% honest if they have to sign their name at the bottom. Also, be very careful who you choose to tally the answers. It might make sense for the Office Manager to do it, but what if people have issues with the Office Manager, and everybody knows she will be the one reading their surveys? This might skew the answers, or at a minimum make people very uncomfortable filling out their questionnaire.

Getting the feedback from your staff is usually the easy part. What is not so simple is taking this feedback and using it constructively to improve your workplace. This is particularly true if the survey information brings to light a difficult problem in your ranks. Just rest assured that it is better to know and to do something about it than it is to put your head in the sand.

CHAPTER 14:

What Makes You a Great Boss Anyway?

"Leadership is about making others better as a result of your presence and making sure that impact lasts in your absence"
— Sheryl Sandberg, COO Facebook

We all understand the value of having strong leadership in our organization, but a study by the Stanford Graduate School of Business (*SGSB 2017[13]*) highlights specific character traits and people-management styles that make some bosses better than others. What stood out about this study is not the educational background or business knowledge of the managers who were profiled, but the fact that they shared a common concern for what others thought about them, and a strong desire to mentor others[14].

It takes more than above-average technical and business skills to be a good leader. Traditionally, those with the best technical skills or business acumen are promoted based exclusively on the intuitive recognition of these strengths. Unfortunately, being a great coach and mentor who really cares about others is not something that comes naturally to everyone.

Tech behemoth, Google, commissioned a 2011 study titled "Eight Habits of Highly Effective Google Managers" which sheds light on the key traits that set a great manager apart from a mediocre one. Based on statistical data gathered from all levels of their organization, what they came up with sounds very much like the exact same principles which would describe a good manager at every other organization in the world. Not surprisingly, the emphasis on strong communication and performance management abilities stand out.

In a nutshell, here are the eight qualities of a great supervisor, as defined by Google:

1. **Be a good coach.**

2. **Empower your team and don't micro-manage.**

3. **Express interest in the team's success and personal well-being.**

4. **Be productive and results-oriented** (set a strong example).

5. **Be a good communicator and listen to your team.**

6. **Help your employees with career development.**

7. **Have a clear vision and strategy for the team.**

8. **Have key technical skills so you can help your team**.

Who can argue with any of these points? However, I feel like I should add in a few of my own. In my experience, having worked closely with leaders of both private and public sector organizations, the best managers also share some of the following characteristics:

1. They believe that employees are the most important contributing factor to the success of the organization, and allow them to take credit when it is due.

2. They approach issues with fairness, build consensus and are open to compromise.

3. They can deal with, and manage, conflict (they do *not* avoid conflict).

4. They provide regular feedback and encourage it in return.

5. They exhibit consistency in behavior and the ability to control their emotions when interacting with staff, while still demonstrating empathy.

6. They are open minded and flexible, with the ability to listen first, and talk later.

7. They can be assertive when they need to be, but are never aggressive.

Don't be disheartened if you are lacking in certain areas. Being a manager is a learning process, and sometimes it takes trial and error (and some disgruntled direct reports) before we are able to fully cultivate the people skills and leadership abilities it takes to effectively support and guide others.

PART IV

The Future of
Performance Management

CHAPTER 15:

What is "Crowd-Sourcing"?

"The competition to hire the best will increase in the years ahead. Companies that give extra flexibility to their employees will have the edge in this area."

— Bill Gates

Funneling feedback to your employees can take many forms, and thanks to Social Media there is now one more way to get this conversation going. Some organizations are using the online world to collect "crowd-source" feedback — a system which allows any employee or manager to give real-time feedback to other employees or supervisors. Unlike traditional performance evaluations, which are usually scheduled, crowd-sourcing is ongoing and allows for the delivery of feedback as projects are in the works.

Jeff Howe and Mark Robinson, editors at Wired Magazine, were among the first to coin the term "crowd-sourcing" in 2005 after noticing the growing trend of businesses using the Internet to outsource work to individuals. Howe and Robinson came to the conclusion that what was happening was like "outsourcing to the crowd," which quickly evolved into the term "crowd-sourcing." Simply defined, crowd-sourcing represents the act of a company or institution taking a function that was once performed by employees and outsourcing it to a network of people in the form of an open call. The project may be taken up by a collaborative group, or by an individual. What is key is that the employer is now choosing from a much larger pool of talent to get the job done.

Since 2005, crowd-sourcing has taken on many different forms in addition to work outplacement, but most relevant to us is its ability to act as a real-time forum for workplace ideas, feedback and problem solving. With many of us now working from home, at branch locations, or in roles which require frequent travel, this provides the opportunity for employees to stay connected with co-workers and with their managers, maintaining a real-time conversation which transcends physical location.

The concept of maintaining these larger-scale connections with professional peers and management has the potential to transform what is thought of as the traditional, one-dimensional performance review. One of the strongest criticisms against performance reviews is that they typically take place only once per year. Social media portals and crowd-sourcing allows for an ongoing stream of discussion, not only between management and employees, but between co-workers as well.

Some say that crowd-sourcing will eventually replace the traditional performance review entirely. I personally don't agree with this. I don't think there is any replacement for sitting down with a person face to face. The quality of that in-person experience will always be greater than a virtual simulation and is vital to ensuring effective organizational development. However, given the emergence of social media technologies as a primary source of communication amongst the current generation entering the workforce, there is no doubt this will play a key role in performance development systems moving forward. This is particularly true if your organization is of a size and scope that does not allow for regular, in-person interaction. On that basis, it is worth embracing and investing in some of the new communication technologies that are emerging.

There are several cloud-based crowd-sourcing software packages suitable for HR applications. You will likely need to work with an IT person who specializes in these mediums as there are more applications and functions involved than I could ever describe here (or understand myself)! As this is a relatively new technology in the world of Human Resources, it will be interesting to see how these communication tools evolve in the years to come. Where it may have faults in terms of lacking direct, one-on-one communication, it has the potential to address some of the shortcomings of the traditional performance evaluation. Collecting feedback from an entire community of peers creates an incredibly powerful development opportunity if implemented in the right way.

With that said, whether your feedback system is documented with a ball-point pen on a piece of paper, or is hosted on an internet social network accessible by Smartphone application, the foundation for an effective Performance Management System remains the same. That you memorialize your conversations with staff about performance and their aspirations is important. How or where you archive this information is not. That's just how we "carry the water," so to speak. The slickest IT solution will not rectify a system that doesn't have the right focus, content and processes to support development in your organization.

Chapter 16:

The Role of Data Analytics, Moving Forward

"Opportunity is missed by most people because it is dressed in overalls and looks like work."

– Thomas Edison

Data analytics is basically the science of making educated conclusions that are based on raw data from a variety of sources. Corporations have been applying analytics to business data for years now, in order to forecast and improve business performance. The principles of this combination of technology and human insight are now being applied to the world of human resources, with mixed results.

According to Josh Bersin (founder of *Bersin by Deloitte)*, who authored a paper in 2013 titled "Managing Talent through Technology," more than 60% of companies are now investing in data analytics tools to help make their HR departments more data-driven. Only 4% of these companies, however, are actually using these tools to their full potential to perform "predictive analytics" about their workforce (ie: understanding what drives performance and retention, studying the correlation between personality traits and job function, using statistics in hiring decisions, analyzing how pay impacts performance, etc.) While the use of these tools for HR purposes is still in the early stages of development, many field experts agree that applying statistical analysis to employee data will be the wave of the future.

While there is certainly a place for the analysis and dissemination of objective data in HR, critics of this system point out the pitfalls of relying too heavily on computerized data to make judgments on hiring and personnel issues. First of all, the correlation between random facts about a person such as what websites they visit and how they like to spend their free time have questionable relevance to whether or not they will succeed in a certain job function. Ever since the invention of the IQ Test, it has been proven time and time again that a person's thought processes are not fail-proof indicators of success.

Just because data analytics seems to work well as a marketing tool (i.e. using mega stores of abstract data to determine what products people will buy), can it really be used as a replacement for observing employees in a real-world setting?

For data analytics to work in an HR context, you need to start with a significant database of employee information, which may include anything from peer reviews and staff surveys, to performance appraisals and sales reports. You then need to convert this to empirical data. The goal is to take this data and use it to find commonalities among your top performers, perhaps pinpoint areas of employee dissatisfaction, and ultimately come up with viable models for employee retention and growth.

Many organizations have traditionally relied on instinct in their decision making processes – to shift from this paradigm to one that is centered around the analytical review of raw data is challenging conventional HR. While IBM and SAP (among others) offer user-friendly "Big Data" software packages, it is not enough to just compile the data, you must know what to do with the data once they have it. For this reason, many companies are relying on the help of outside experts to make sense out of what can be an overwhelming store of information.

While there are inherent flaws to this system, there are examples of companies that have used data analytics with great success. Google is the premier example of a company that has used its massive analytics database and applied it to every HR function from compensation to talent management. Their HR department is data-driven. Keep in mind, Google has an entire team of HR staffers devoted solely to analytics! Their People Analytics Team studies a combination of performance review data and employee surveys to come up with conclusions on what working styles make the best bosses, forecasts on future organizational structure, which hiring and promotion practices have been the most effective, and numerous other projects.

Not that long ago, their People Analytics Team came up with the conclusion that if Google continued to promote at its current rate, it would end up with too many mid-ranking employees and fewer opportunities for junior hires to advance[15]. Google subsequently implemented a new practice where, instead of directly filling vacancies through the traditional means, they bring in new hires at a lower level and develop them into more senior roles. The People Analytics Team forecasted that this would make career advancement easier for junior employees, and improve the perception that Google offers long-term advancement opportunities to those who are worthy.

Google must be doing something right, because their analytics system is currently considered one of the best examples in the world of how to incorporate data-driven people management into an HR structure. Perhaps the secret to their success is best described by Kathryn Dekas, Manager of Google's People Analytics Team, who has been quoted as saying *"You can't have an algorithm for everything. You use data to inform, but you don't rely on the data to make the decision."*

The key, it seems, is to use the data as a reference point, but not as the sole means of HR planning. At the end of the day you must still make educated choices which are practical and sensible for your business and your people.

CHAPTER 17:

What are the Biggest HR Mistakes You're Making Right Now?

"I have not failed. I've just found 10,000 ways that won't work."
                                                              – Thomas Edison

When we go into companies with struggling management and HR departments, or smaller businesses that perhaps have no formal HR structure at all, I see many similarities. I am often asked by these clients what they are doing wrong from an HR perspective, and how they can get their programming on track. In most cases, there are common mistakes being made that are quite easy to iron out.

Below is a list of what I consider to be the biggest HR pitfalls I see on a regular basis. Without these elements in place, it will be challenging to implement the performance management strategies I have outlined in this book. Think of these as the basic foundation upon which your organization's HR strategy should be built:

❖ **Have accurate, well-written job descriptions.** You won't set the world on fire creating thoughtful, precise job descriptions, but having this information properly organized should be a foundational priority in all organizations despite what the neo-HR / anti-HR experts may say to the contrary.

I know your business is growing, everyone is busy, who has time to sit down and write comprehensive job profiles for every position in your organization? Unfortunately, without this critical HR foundation in place, employees may not be sure exactly what their day to day tasks are, and it also makes it difficult to intentionally develop performance and benchmark expectations. Before you move forward with more sophisticated organizational development, make sure you have this baseline information clearly defined and established in your organization.

❖ **Don't botch the recruiting process!** I continue to be surprised that so many businesses choose to recruit without a structured process in place. The most effective development process in the world will not compensate for poor hiring choices. If you recruit mission-appropriate staff you have an excellent opportunity to engage their talents and to promote your development as an organization. Once you have perfected the interview process and have narrowed the candidates down to two or three, don't rush an offer. No matter how anxious you are to get someone on board, make sure you have engaged in a thorough process which includes multiple interviews with key members of your team and some form of behavioral-based assessment. You must always check references from former employers, and conduct a thorough background check. Though it is not a central focus of this book, I cannot over-emphasize the importance of recruiting the right people. Some of our clients impress with their extensive investment in leadership and skills training. That's all good. But if you carefully hire for these skills and aptitudes from the out-set, you can avoid the long and occasionally unfruitful exercise of trying to embed and grow these characteristics in staff who may not be readily able to perform accordingly.

I'm not saying you shouldn't invest in your people. In fact, this is essential to the success of a High Performance Work System and will contribute to engagement and staff development. What I am recommending is that if you have the opportunity to recruit, don't short-circuit the process or settle just to get the chair filled. Take pause, evaluate your needs and then go find someone who meets these requirements so that you're investing your training and development resources into top-grading your staff's potential, rather than addressing gaps in technical skills, motivation and leadership ability. Some of these shortcomings may be very difficult to ameliorate with even the best training.

❖ **Have a step-by-step process in place for documenting performance issues.** Don't wait until you have a problem with an employee before coming up with some kind of system for managing the situation. Make it known to your staff, and then follow it. And, as outlined earlier, don't torpedo your *performance development* process with discussions about corrective action. The main thing to remember is that you should have a fair system for documenting behavior that falls short of expectations. Every manager on your team should be aware of the system and know what steps to take as problem situations occur. Employees must know where they stand and you can only achieve this by sharing feedback on a regular basis. Give employees the opportunity to improve and correct their behavior and job performance. Without that basic level of procedural fairness, you will instill a culture of uncertainty and instability. Your system must be completely transparent and structured as a corrective process, not as a disciplinary one.

❖ **Have at least a basic knowledge of employment regulations.** If you think that certain employment laws don't apply to you, perhaps because you have a very small business or operate as a not-for-profit, then you're wrong. You don't need to be an expert in this area (you have a business to run), but you must understand the basics. If you don't have the time or resources to fully inform yourself about all of the rules-of-the-road, make sure you have a reliable expert you can consult as exceptional issues arise.

❖ **Every business needs an Employee Handbook.** As with job descriptions, the creation and regular updating of an Employee Handbook is a project that often gets swept under the rug. It's the sort of thing that no one really thinks of until there's a problem. Of course you have norms, rules and policies in your workplace, but unless they're written down they just don't count for much. An employee handbook acts as a reference for every member of your staff, from entry-level employees to senior management, and should be presented to each incumbent on their first day of work. No one will be able to say they "didn't know" because they have been given fair access to all the rules for conduct and behavior in your workplace, clearly laid out in black and white. I can't overemphasize the importance of your employee handbook being professionally organized and well written. There must be the perception that this is an official document if you want it to be taken seriously. As with your job descriptions, this should be a foundation point in your organization.

CHAPTER 18:

Critics of Performance Management

In the interest of presenting an unbiased view on performance management, I will end where I began to share the opinion of critics out there who feel that performance reviews, constructive feedback and related programming don't really do anything to improve actual employee performance.

In an article in the *Harvard Business Review (November 2013)*, Tony Schwartz, President and CEO of the Energy Project, and author of *Be Excellent At Anything,* says that when we hear the phrase from someone, "would you mind if I give you some feedback?" what that actually means to most of us is "would you mind if I give you some *negative* feedback?" You can call it constructive, but criticism is criticism, any way you want to package it.

Schwartz contends that criticism "challenges our sense of value. Criticism implies judgment and we all recoil from feeling judged." Our brains are wired to protect our ego from attack, and any perception of personal negativity threatens our very sense of self.

I'm not a psychologist, but numerous articles have been written in *Psychology Today* on this very topic. Ray Williams, a regular contributor to *Psychology Today* and author of the popular blog, *Wired for Success*[16], argues that "nowhere does negative or constructive criticism appear more frequently than in performance reviews of employees. The prevailing theory is that criticism, which invariably is part of the performance review, will improve the employee's performance, and in addition the employee will positively welcome it. Nothing can be further from the truth."

He goes on to opine that the traditional performance appraisal as practiced in the majority of organizations today is fundamentally flawed, and incongruent with our values-based, vision-driven and collaborative work environments.

There are some studies which back up what Williams is saying. A 2005 national U.S. survey by the consulting firm, People IQ, found that 87 percent of employees and managers felt performance reviews were neither useful nor effective, and that at least 30 percent of performance reviews ended up decreasing employee performance. The same study showed that 60% of HR Executives graded their Performance Management system a "C" or below. This is not an encouraging response from a leadership group which should be flag-bearers for engagement and development progress.

We cannot argue with the statistical evidence that many performance management systems in organizations today are simply not producing the intended results. However, I have also noticed that critics of performance management do not often provide a viable alternative to developing staff performance. While many organizations fall short in terms of their employee review processes, having a *laissez faire* attitude of simply hoping that everyone gets their job done with minimal input, and no feedback, is not going to work either.

When implemented properly, performance management can do amazing things for your organizational culture. When handled poorly, it can have the opposite effect, derailing your employees and causing widespread dissatisfaction. Even the best systems on paper can have negative repercussions if carried out in a counterproductive manner. As we've already detailed earlier in the book, there are five common mistakes that can disrupt your performance development program:

1. **Implementing an overly ambitious system.** It is important to create a performance development strategy that is easily understood by your staff, with goals that are challenging but realistically attainable. Your system should take into account and encourage employee autonomy. In order for productivity to increase in the long-term, your team needs to know that you trust them to get the job done without having to constantly measure every detail of their performance.

2. **Failing to engage your employees.** For any organizational initiative to succeed, it must involve considerable feedback and input from your staff. This is the only way that they will take ownership of your plan and run with it. It is up to you and your frontline managers to keep the conversation ongoing: *How can we make this plan better? What do you need from us to achieve these*

goals? We want your input on next steps we should take to make this happen!

3. **Focusing only on shortcomings.** If there is one surefire way to de-motivate your staff, it is to focus only on what they're doing wrong. Use any opportunity to highlight their strengths and further develop areas that they have a natural propensity to achieve in. Do not look at your employees as people who need to be "fixed". Being successful in the workplace commonly starts by taking a dominant talent and gradually building out other skills and knowledge through training and experience.

4. **Not monitoring your system on a continual basis.** It's important to continuously review and improve your performance development strategy with ongoing feedback. Once strategic plans and performance metrics have been established, this is really only the beginning. Managers and those reporting to them must be trained in how to organize effective performance discussions, and how to encourage development on an ongoing basis to ensure professional growth. Most importantly, feedback should be constructive and continuous – do not wait until a designated appraisal time to dialogue with your staff.

5. **Having a negative-incentive system.** We're afraid of failure but sometimes need to fail to achieve success. If there is a perception among your workforce that they will receive penalties for not achieving set goals, this can be very damaging to morale. Instead, accept, embrace and encourage "failures" – your team will never innovate if you don't give them

the freedom to fail and the security to experiment in a safe environment. James Dyson made 5,127 attempts over 15 years before engineering the bagless vacuum. Success doesn't typically come easily or quickly.

The approach I have outlined in this book is all about focusing on the positive when it comes to development - and development must be your goal if your intention is to create a system that inspires engagement and organizational effectiveness. In my experience, people are much more open to fully participating in development programs if they have assurances that the process is just that: developmental. Once you introduce significant chunks of "constructive feedback" into a performance review session, you undermine and diminish the development potential of your discussion. Employees disengage from those processes. Always.

With some employees, you may have to look a little bit harder to find the positive, but that is your job as a leader: bringing out the best in a person and further developing these qualities in their day-to-day work. Leveraging strength drives performance.

Yes, human beings do have fragile egos, but I also believe that employees who are looking to improve themselves professionally are eager to take the necessary steps to make this happen. If you have followed all the steps of conducting an effective performance discussion and have been met with a poor attitude and reluctance to change or adapt, it may be time to re-read Chapter 11! Performance development is all about reaching out to those members of your team who want to be at work every day. If you have made every effort to create a positive environment and deliver feedback in the manner that has been outlined in this program, but you still have an employee who is non-responsive, then this person might not be the right fit for your organization. It happens.

Managers must also be conscious of providing ongoing feedback, while still fostering self direction. This can be a tricky tight-rope. How much feedback is too much? When should you just step back and let the employees take over? It takes considerable judgment and managerial finesse to answer these questions, which is why not everyone is cut out to be a leader! For your performance culture to take root, and not fall victim to the fate prophesied by its critics, you must strike a balance between nurturing your team, and knowing when to give the autonomy that everyone ultimately needs to take their job and run with it. Only you will know when it is appropriate to step in, and when it is time to step back.

The Future

The conventional annual appraisal process is evolving, and for the better. Consulting and Professional Service firm giants such as Accenture and Deloitte, which have embraced performance management for decades, are swapping out those traditional systems in favor of more fluid, real-time feedback opportunities that may follow the completion of a client project or engagement.

Millennials want to know how they're doing *now*. They are less interested in a rear-way conversation about what happened six months ago or last year. Future performance, and how to get there, is more important in these workplaces than retrospectives on past performance. This dynamic also creates opportunities for employees and their leaders to interact and collaborate on initiatives that can have impact on current projects and challenges, as opposed to being solely focused on a "performance appraisal" for the sake of that process alone.

Living in a "real-time" culture that has been facilitated and perpetuated by technology makes the need for ongoing and timely dialogue with staff that much more relevant. Thankfully, communication technologies have made it easier than ever to keep the conversation going, even for those managers and business owners who spend a considerable amount of time traveling and who might otherwise lose a sense of what is happening in their workplace on a day-to-day basis. Regardless of how you choose to keep the lines of communication open, the goal is for performance development to be a continuous process, or *habit,* rather than a once-a-year event.

Appendices

Case Study - Performance Objective Scenario (Carl)

- Carl is the newest employee in a medium-sized medical devices manufacturer owned by a local family. He is a recent graduate of a community college, life sciences program and was hired on the recommendation of one of the owner's children who played competitive-level hockey with Carl during their time in high school together.

- Carl performs work to an acceptable level, only. He is cooperative with coworkers and produces reasonable work, usually with some minor errors. Work is most often, but not always finished on time – but just in time, consistently at the "11th hour".

- Carl does the minimum required, showing no extra effort or commitment to his work, or his own development as an employee.

- Provide Feedback to Carl.

Case Study Solution - Performance Objective Scenario (Carl)

Performance Plan

- Employees in this category may be more difficult to set objectives for, and provide feedback to, as their performance technically meets minimum standards.

- But this is perhaps where Goal-setting, Effective Feedback and a development discussion can have the greatest impact since there are no "conduct" issues and an opportunity exists to develop performance and foster greater productivity.

- Therefore, the focus of your discussion should be more of a coaching exercise.

- Start with positive feedback first (emphasize strengths and build on those achievements to drive performance).

- Ask the employee what they think they could do to improve performance (leave the onus with them to suggest solutions – don't become their personal problem-solver. Do they need resources, a training plan?)

- Tap into their personal and career-goals.

- Set quantifiable goals s/he can work toward (i.e. meeting a certain production target each week, or providing a certain number of reports each quarter - whatever is relevant in your organization).

- Achievable, quantifiable goals are a good place to start with 'underachievers' to promote initial successes that can be built upon to encourage motivation and improvement, and to set the stage for the achievement of more progressive or complex performance objectives.

- If needed, set deadline goals to ensure timeliness is improved.

- Set some stretch-goals together (its important to have involvement, consensus and buy-in from the employee – don't just dictate the goals yourself).

- Tie those goals to recognition and rewards.

- Suggest opportunities for training or development.

- Confirm that their contributions are important to the team and that their success as an individual is key to the organization's overall success.

- Follow-up with regular feedback and check-ins with the employee.

Remember: Follow 3 Basic Rules for Setting Performance Objectives:

1. Identify the Performance **Objective** (Goal or Target)

2. Agree on a **Measurement** Criteria

3. Establish a Deadline, Outcome or Target for Review (**DOT** your Goals !)

Case Study - Feedback Scenario One (Shirley)

- Shirley has the most seniority in a social services organization and has been in the same position for nearly 20 years. Over the course of the last several months, she has been acting in an aggressive, uncooperative manner at work: Co-workers find her difficult and unapproachable.

- Her Manager has met with her several times – initially, "off-the-record" as a personal gesture to reach-out to Shirley, based on their long working relationship and given her loyalty within the agency. Nonetheless, efforts to extend assistance and to provide feedback have proven ineffective and the Manager, partially in frustration has told Shirley to "...*just get your job done and get over your personal baggage.*"

- Following these dialogues and this particular comment, Shirley makes an allegation of harassment against her Manager, claiming among other things, that she's been singled-out for these discussions and that no other employees have been subjected to the same treatment. The harassment allegation is eventually resolved, however Shirley's performance continues to deteriorate.

- Provide Feedback to Shirley.

Case Study Solution - Feedback Scenario One (Shirley)

Performance Plan

- Performance and personal conduct are among the most difficult issues to address.

- Deal with aggressive behaviors immediately before they escalate.

- Deal with aggressive behavior and personal misconduct when it happens, or shortly thereafter (do not save it for an "annual" review).

- Use Root Cause Analysis to assess the situation:

  o carefully evaluate why there is a failure

  o is it a performance issue or a personal conduct issue ?

- Sometimes root causes have nothing to do with the workplace (ie. alcoholism, personal, marital issues).

- Do not provide counsel for personal issues (you can recommend resources, but you are not a counselor).

- You are not responsible for resolving personal issues, but as a Manager, you are responsible for setting expectations for behavior and performance in the workplace – and offering the resources and support to the employee (but they are responsible for achievement, not you).

- Always focus on the issue, the conduct or the objective desired – never the *person*.

- Do not react to emotional behavior – nor should you take "attacks" personally.

- If the climate of the discussion escalates to a point where constructive dialogue is no longer possible – park the conversation, and resume after a period of reflection.

- Stick to facts and observations – do not draw conclusions, lecture or condescend to the employee.

- Ask them for their ideas about how they can improve their performance or address the situation.

- Take those ideas and document goals, or an improvement plan.

- If constructive feedback and coaching fails, develop a formal Personal Improvement Plan to correct behavior.

Follow 4 Basic Rules for providing **Feedback**:

1. Focus on the conduct, issue (the **Objective**), not the Person

2. Be **Specific** about what you've observed

3. Have a **Constructive** purpose for the Feedback

4. Provide **Specific** suggestions for improvement

   (Ask the Employee for solutions, first)

Case Study - Feedback Scenario Two (Karen)

- Karen is a Project Manager in a growing Consulting Engineering firm that provides services to industrial and municipal clients. She is a classic "over-achiever" who frequently receives performance bonuses based on the impact of her work.

160

- She spends long hours at the office and produces an exceptional amount of work at a consistently high level of quality. With that said, there are some areas of concern. She is a high detail-person and sometimes focuses too much on fine points which can unnecessarily delay the completion of a project or task for others who depend on her to complete project tasks before they can move forward with their own work.

- Karen is also "short" with co-workers who don't work at her level (prefers working alone than on teams). She dismisses company procedures that she doesn't agree with as "bureaucracy" and can be abrasive with working on team projects, disregarding the input and opinions of colleagues on the team.

- Provide Feedback to Karen.

Case Study - Feedback Scenario Two (Karen)

Performance Plan

- Overachievers in particular need feedback to keep them motivated. Feedback is good for everyone!

- Generously praise them for the good work done to reinforce the positive.

- Communication is key.

- However, high output staff can be difficult to manage, and need feedback on how to better interact and communicate with peers. Most work is a team sport, and relationships with colleagues are important and need to be respected, and strengthened whenever possible.

- Overachievers need coaching to improve listening skills, cooperation and collaboration with coworkers.

- Create, reinforce and reward teamwork opportunities.

- Consider team incentives to reinforce that behavior vs. individual recognition.

- Give candid and specific feedback.

- Recognize the *results* of work, rather than time spent working on the project to minimize too much focus on details.

- Don't tolerate aggressive behavior in your workplace (cursing, yelling, door slamming). Address it constructively and immediately. Always.

- Deal with aggressive behaviors immediately before they escalate.

- Set boundaries for all team members to follow in meetings and other discussions – and eject people from meetings if necessary should these boundaries be crossed.

- Monitor work-life balance issues. Imbalances can cause issues: if the employee is spending too much time at work, this can cause fatigue (burnout), diminish performance, and increase irritability. Ensure time is taken to refresh and gain perspective.

Endnote References

[1] Hard Facts, Dangerous Half-Truths, and Total Nonsense: Profiting from Evidence-based Management, by Jeffrey Pfeffer & Robert I. Sutton, Harvard Business Press, 2006

[2] WorldatWork/Sibson 2010 Study on The State of Performance Management

[3] Global Performance Management Survey, Mercer LLC, 2013

[4] Managing Human Resources: Productivity, Quality of Work Life, Profits, Wayne Cascio, McGraw Hill, 2006.

[5] Retaining Talent: Replacing Misconceptions With Evidence-Based Strategies, by David G. Allen, Phillip C. Bryant, and James M. Vardaman, Academy of Management Perspectives, May 2008

[6] Worldwide, 13% of Employees Are Engaged at Work, Steve Crabtree, Gallup World, October 2013

[7] Source: Statistics Canada

[8] Drive, Daniel H. Pink, Penguin Books, 2011

9   Split Roles in Performance Appraisal, Herbert H. Meyer, Emanuel Kay, and John R. P. French, Jr., Harvard Business Journal, January 1965

10   "A Theory of Human Motivation", Abraham Maslow, The Psychological Review, 1943

11   "One More Time: How Do You Motivate Employees?", Frederick Herzberg, Harvard Business Review, January 1968.

12   Pygmalion in the Classroom: Teacher Expectation and Pupils' Intellectual Development, Robert Rosenthal and Lenore Jacobson, Crown House Publishing Limited, 1968.

13   *Pygmalion in Management*, J. Sterling Livingston, Harvard Business Review, 1969 (*reproduced in 2003*).

14   How to be a Good Boss in a Bad Economy, Robert I. Sutton, Harvard Business Review, June 2009

15   Source: Analysis of Google HR Strategy, DocStoc, February 2012

16   Wired for Success is a blog that focuses on workplace issues of leadership, organization, employee motivation and engagement, https://www.psychologytoday.com/blog/wired-success

About the Author

Matthew Savino is the Managing Partner of SHRP Limited, a Canadian management consulting firm that supports the HR and organizational requirements of both private and public sector clients. He is also Co-Founder of HRLive, a Software-as-a-Service (SaaS) company dedicated to meeting the Human Resources needs of organizations with timely, effective HR support. Matthew has 20 years of business and HR leadership experience as a  Director and Vice-President of Human Resources in a number of Canadian and international companies. Matthew holds degrees in Economics (B.A.) and Law (LL.B.) as well as certificates in Dispute Resolution & Mediation, and is a certified Leadership Development Trainer. He is a member of the Human Resources Professionals Association (HRPA) and is recognized as a Certified Human Resources Executive (CHRE).

For more information about SHRP Ltd or HRLive, please visit our websites at www.savinohrp.ca and www.HRLive.ca

Made in the USA
Middletown, DE
27 June 2019